Intellectual Property Handbook

Michael A. Lechter

TechPress, Inc.
An affiliate of Meyer, Hendricks, Victor, Osborn & Maledon, P.A.
Phoenix, Arizona

Intellectual Property Handbook

© Copyright 1991, 1994 Michael A. Lechter
All rights reserved. No part of this book shall be produced, stored in a retrieval system, or transmitted by any means, electronic, mechanical, photocopying, recording or otherwise, without written permission from the publisher. No patent liability is assumed with respect to the use of the information contained herein. Although every precaution has been taken in the preparation of this book, the publisher and the author assume no responsibility for errors or omissions. Neither is any liability assumed for damages resulting from the use of the information contained herein. For information, contact TechPress, Inc., Post Office Box 33449, Phoenix, AZ 85067-3449.

Library of Congress Catalog Card Number 94-61489

ISBN 0-9643856-0-0

Printed in the United States.

TABLE OF CONTENTS

Introduction	v
The Basic Categories of Intellectual Property	1
Information, Data, and Know-How	2
Inventions	3
Industrial Designs	3
Patents	3
Utility Model (Petty Patent)	4
Copyrights	4
Mask Works	5
Trademarks, Reputation, and Goodwill	5
Character Trademarks and Sponsorship	6
Trade Dress	6
The Basic Protection Mechanisms	7
Trade Secret Protection	9
Scope of Protection	10
Procedure for Maintaining a Trade Secret	11
Exploiting Trade Secrets	13
Special Consideration with Respect to Software Developments	13
Patent Protection	17
Utility Patent Protection	17
Exclusive Right	18
Ownership of a Patent	20
Recording of Assignments, Grants, and Conveyances	20
Patentable Subject Matter; Applicability to Software Inventions	21
Statutory Bars	26
Prior Public Knowledge	26
Premature Disclosure or Sale	27
Patented	28
Described in a Printed Publication	28
Public Use	29
On Sale	30
Strict Novelty in Most Foreign Countries	31
Abandonment	32
Corresponding Foreign Patent Applications	32
Actual Inventor	33
First to Make the Invention	35
Obviousness	38

The Procedure for Obtaining Patent Protection	39
Confidentiality	39
State-of-the-Art Search	39
Assessing Patentability	39
Disclosure Materials	40
Infringement Search	41
Preparing the Application	42
The Patent Application	42
Prosecution Before the Patent and Trademark Office	48
Design Patent Protection	49
Enforcing a Patent	50
Remedies for Patent Infringement	51
Post Issuance Actions	53
Reexamination	53
Advantages of Obtaining a Patent	54
Practical Considerations with Respect to Software Inventions	55

Copyright Protection   57

Ownership of a Copyright	58
Scope of Protection	60
The Fair Use Limitation	61
Limitations on the Scope of Copyright Protection of Software	62
Practical Considerations with Respect to Software Works	63
Right to Make Archival and Transitory Copies	66
Fair Use as Applied to Computer Programs	67
Publication	67
Notice	67
Term	68
Deposit	69
Registration	69
Procedure for Obtaining a Registration	69

Trademark Protection   73

Acquiring Rights	74
Choosing a Mark	75
"Confusingly Similar"	77
Federal Registration	78
Registering a Trademark	82
Contesting Registration: Opposition and Cancellation Proceedings	86
Trademark Marking	87
Post Registration Actions	88
Term of the Registration	88
Maintaining Trademark Rights	88
State Anti-Dilution Statutes	89
Practical Considerations with Respect to Software Goods	89

Mask Work Protection — 91
Protectable Subject Matter; Requisites for Protection — 92
Scope of Protection — 93
Notice — 95
Term; Registration — 95
Enforcement; Remedies — 95
Practical Considerations — 96

Comparison of the Protection Mechanisms — 97

Suggested Procedures — 103
Securing and Maintaining Rights in Technology — 103
- Employee Non-Disclosure and Non-Use Agreements — 103
- Preliminary State of the Art Investigation — 103
- Initially Keep R & D as a Trade Secret — 104
- Maintain Documentation — 104
- Timely Consideration of Patent Protection — 104
- Infringement Clearance Procedure — 105

Keeping Accurate Records — 105
- Need for Keeping Accurate Records — 105
- Development and Government Contracts — 106
- License Agreements — 106
- Confidentiality and Non-Use Agreements — 107
- Prior Development Defense to Patent Infringement and Interface Proceedings — 107
- The Two-Step Process of "Making an Invention" — 108
- Record Keeping Procedures — 108
- Preliminary Concept Report Form — 109
- Notebooks — 109
- Time Records — 111
- Conclusion — 111

Securing and Maintaining Rights in Trademarks — 111
- Choice of a Mark — 111
- Use the Mark as a Source Indicator — 112
- General Rules — 112

Procedures for Avoiding Potential Infringement of Third-Party Intellectual Property Rights — 115
- Avoiding Infringement of Third Party Trade Secret Rights — 115
- Avoiding Infringement of Third Party Patents — 116
- Avoiding Infringement of Third Party Copyrights — 117
- Avoiding Infringement of Third Party Trademark Rights — 117
- Avoiding Infringement of Third Party Mask Work Registrations — 118

Overview and Comparison of Agreements Affecting Intellectual Property Rights and Liabilities — 119
- Agreements Regarding Transfers of Rights — 119
  - Assignments — 120
  - License Agreements: In General — 120
  - Patent Licenses — 122
  - Know-How Licenses — 122
  - Trademark Licenses — 122
  - Franchise Agreements — 123
  - Technical Services and Assistance Agreements — 123
  - Hybrid License Agreements — 123
- Agreements Regarding Internal Relationships — 124
  - Employee Agreements as to Confidentiality and Ownership of Intellectual Property — 124
  - Non-Competition Agreements — 124
- Agreements Regarding Third Party Business Relationships — 124
  - Confidentiality Agreements — 125
  - Consulting and Development Agreements — 125
  - Maintenance and Support Agreements — 126
  - Manufacturing Agreements — 126
  - Joint Ventures — 127
- Agreements Regarding Sales and Market Relationships — 127
  - Purchase Agreements — 127
  - Distribution Agreements — 128
  - VAR and OEM Agreements — 129
- Some Basic Considerations in Negotiating Agreements — 130
  - The Principle of Reasonableness — 130
  - The Principle of Definiteness — 130
  - The Principle of Completeness — 130
- The Periodic Intellectual Property Audit — 131

Conclusion — 133

Appendices
APPENDIX I
   Comparison of U.S. Intellectual Property Protection Mechanisms
APPENDIX II
   Procedure for Protecting Intellectual Property
APPENDIX III
   Search Request Disclosure
APPENDIX IV
   Invention Disclosure

Introduction

The term "intellectual property" covers a broad gamut of intangible assets. It is widely recognized that these intangible assets include patents, copyrights, mask works, and trademarks. Intellectual property, however, also includes such things as trade dress, goodwill, and reputation. It also includes expertise, data, know-how, and other information regarding business subjects (such as management and operations, marketing and sales) and technology. It can be the collective knowledge and expertise of a company or that of individual employees. Creating and maintaining rights in such intellectual property, and avoiding infringement of the intellectual property rights of others, are becoming an increasingly important aspect of the professional activities of the practicing technologist, manager, and entrepreneur.

This handbook is designed to familiarize the reader with the basic mechanisms for protecting rights in technology and other intellectual property. The characteristics and relative advantages of each protection mechanism will be discussed, as will the basic procedures for obtaining, maintaining, and exploiting rights through these mechanisms.

At the outset, however, it must be stressed that this handbook is *not* intended to be an exhaustive treatise on the subject. There are many subtleties involved in establishing and protecting rights in technology that are totally beyond the scope of this handbook. *This handbook will not turn the reader into an "instant attorney."* What this handbook will do, however, is alert the reader to the pitfalls that can strip the rights from the unwary.

Example 1:

Ackman developed a new video game conceptually different from all previous video games. In addition to the conceptual differences from previous games, this game program employed radically new data manipulation techniques which permitted generation of 3-D images using a standard color cathode ray tube. Ackman began marketing the game software both in ROM "cartridge" and disc form. Each article sold was dutifully marked with a copyright notice.

The game was an instant success and the programming technique was proclaimed a major breakthrough. Within a matter of months, competing games, conceptually the same as Ackman's game, but employing different audiovisual effects and minor functional differences, began to appear. Ackman sued for copyright infringement. Ackman lost.

Ackman also learned that a number of companies were employing his 3-D display programming techniques in other products and games. His attorney advised him that his copyright provided no recourse and that he should have obtained patent protection on his program. Ackman learned the hard way that a copyright provides only a very limited form of protection.

Example 2:

After years of R & D, Z-Corp. developed a revolutionary new micro computer that had taken the market by storm. After only a little more than one year on the market, Z-Corp.'s product literally became the premium micro on the market. Suddenly, sales began to drop. Z-Corp. learned that Copy Co. purchased, then copied, a Z-Corp. unit and is now marketing a competing product. The Copy Co. unit differs from the Z-Corp. product only in the details of the casing and the unmistakable "Copy Co." decal on the front of the unit. However, since Copy Co. has essentially no research and development costs to recoup, the Copy Co. unit is being sold at a substantially lower price. At this point, Z-Corp. for the first time seeks legal advice on how to protect its R & D investment. Z-Corp. is out of luck.

Example 3:

Dr. A is employed by Y-Corp. in its R & D section and has developed a new semiconductor device with phenomenal frequency characteristics. Dr. A, eager to receive credit for developing the new device, immediately publishes a technical paper. Within the next few months, Y-Corp. perceives that the primary market for the new device is in Japan and Germany, and attempts to protect its rights in the device in those countries. Y-Corp. is too late for patent protection in those countries.

Example 4:

Ms. B had an idea for a new system architecture, and jotted down notes and a diagram on a piece of scrap paper, without signing or dating the paper. A few months later, Ms. B approached her employers to see if they were interested in manufacturing a system using her architecture. Her employers immediately saw great potential for the architecture, and agreed to pay Ms. B a substantial sum for rights to the architecture, if they were successful in obtaining a patent. A patent application was immediately filed in Ms. B's name, and the Patent and Trademark Office determined that the architecture was indeed patentable. However, a third party had also developed a similar architecture, and had also filed a patent application. An "interference proceeding" was instituted in the Patent and Trademark Office to determine who was entitled to claim the invention of the system architecture. It soon became evident to Ms. B that she was the first to have the idea. Unfortunately, she had no way of proving it, and the third party was awarded the patent.

Example 5:

Mr. X is president of X-Corp., a service company that lays out and manufactures custom PC-boards. X-Corp. has developed a new computer-aided technique and necessary software that permits it to substantially increase the density of components per unit area on a PC-board as compared to the products of its closest competitor. In attempting to obtain a substantial order from a potential customer, Mr. X explained the new technique and software in detail to the potential customer without reservation. Later, after it appeared that X-Corp. could not meet all of the customer's demands, the customer placed a second order with one of X-Corp.'s fiercest competitors, and, in the course of doing so, explained the X-Corp. technique and software to the competitor. The competitor thereafter began using X-Corp. techniques in all of its work. X-Corp. lost its edge over the competition.

Example 6:

Z-Corp. spared no expense in rolling out its newest product in December of 1989, and blanketed the market with advertising prominently featuring a catchy trademark. A great deal of thought and expense had gone into the choice of the trademark, and Z-Corp. was certain that no one was using the mark. Unfortunately, Z-Corp. had not thought to do a search of the Patent and Trademark Office files; Agresso Corp. had filed an application for federal registration based upon an intent to use the identical mark just days before Z-Corp.'s roll-out. The notice of trademark infringement caught Z-Corp. completely by surprise.

Example 7:

B. Hindthetimes brought his newest product to market in record time to meet the competition — but he did it without considering his competitor's patent position. He almost immediately received notice from his primary competitor that the new product infringed the competitor's patent. In B. Hindthetimes' opinion, his product did not infringe the patent. In any event, someone had once told him that patents were rarely successfully enforced in the courts. He opted not to consult an attorney and continued to market the product. B. Hindthetimes was soon in court and found himself faced with an injunction and a judgment for treble damages plus attorneys' fees. B. Hindthetimes learned the hard way that patents are now very enforceable in the courts, and that he would have been well served to have consulted a patent attorney before he went to market.

* * *

These hypotheticals are typical examples of how valuable rights in "intellectual property" are unwittingly lost by seemingly innocent courses of action, and how failing to consider third party rights can lead to disaster.

The Basic Categories of Intellectual Property

It is important to have some familiarity with the various types of intellectual property. The major categories of intellectual property include information, data and know-how, inventions, industrial designs, patents, utility models, copy-

> **The Different Types of Intellectual Property**
> - Information, Data, and Know-How
> - Inventions and Patents
> - Industrial Designs and Design Patents
> - Patents
> - Utility Model
> - Copyrights
> - Mask Works
> - Trademarks, Reputation, and Goodwill
> - Character Trademarks and Sponsorships

rights, mask works, trademarks, reputation and goodwill.[1] The nature, applicability, and scope of legal protection mechanisms for the different types of intellectual properties will be noted, but discussed in more detail in the next section.

---

[1] As will be discussed in the next section, the terms trade secrets, patents, copyrights, mask works, and trademarks have come to denote both a type of intellectual property asset and a legal mechanism for protecting the underlying assets.

Information, Data, and Know-How

Perhaps the most overlooked or undervalued intellectual property assets are accumulated information, data, and know-how. There is no universally accepted term that describes these assets, nor is there a universally accepted definition of the term "know-how." For the purposes of this handbook, however, know-how will be used as a generic term, generally defined as accumulated practical skill, expertise, data, and information relating to a company and its operations, or performing any form of industrial procedure or process. Examples of business know-how include such things as strategic business plans, marketing plans, internal procedures, sales techniques, and client lists. Examples of technological know-how may include manufacturing processes, vendor and parts lists, inventions, technical developments, and skill and expertise in operating equipment and instrumentation. Know-how may be either proprietary or non-proprietary.

> **Know-How**
> Accumulated practical skill, expertise, data, and information.

"Non-proprietary know-how" is information which is generally known in an industry, or basic skills or practices employed in an industry. A typical example would be the skills and knowledge acquired by an employee resulting from being trained in the operation of a commercially available machine (as opposed to learning a trade secret process). There is clearly an investment by the company in training the employee; even this non-proprietary know-how can be an asset, as will be discussed.

"Proprietary know-how," sometimes referred to as a "trade secret" or "confidential information," is know-how which could only be obtained, if at all, other than from the owner of the know-how, with a substantial effort and expenditure of time and money. As will be discussed, to be subject to an enforceable trade secret right, the know-how must not be generally known in the industry, must be subject to appropriate measures to maintain its secrecy, and may not be disclosed to any entity that is not also obligated to maintain the know-how in confidence.

Know-how can be embodied in many forms. It can be business or technical documents such as strategic plans, customer lists and files, specifications, manuals, blueprints, and the like. It can also reside in the personal knowledge and expertise of employees.

Non-proprietary know-how can be best protected by retaining employees. As will be discussed, non-competition provisions are sometimes used to prevent competitors from appropriating a company's investment in employee training. However, such agreements with employees are often difficult to enforce. Establishing procedures for recording the details of processes, methods, techniques, and data used by skilled employees, and for retaining possession of those records, also accords a modicum of protection; at least the know-how would not be entirely lost should the employee leave.

As will be discussed in more detail, rights in proprietary know-how are typically maintained through physical security procedures and by imposing a contractual obligation of confidentiality on all parties permitted access to the know-how. The obligation of confidentiality is typically imposed through appropriate provisions in confidentiality, employment, development, supply/vender, manufacturing, foundry, and license agreements. Non-competition agreements are also sometimes employed to prevent inevitable disclosure of trade secrets by former employees.

Inventions

> **Invention**
> New technology or developments produced through independent creative thought, investigation, or experimentation.

In general, "inventions" are new technological developments or discoveries produced or created through the exercise of independent creative thought, investigation, or experimentation. Inventions may constitute know-how (typically trade secrets) and be protected as such or may be the subject of patents granted by the governments of various countries.

Industrial Designs

The term "industrial design" tends to mean different things from country to country. In general, however, "industrial design" typically refers to the appearance and nonfunctional aspects of a product. The scope of protection granted with respect to industrial design varies from country to country. In the United States, industrial designs typically are protected by design patents.

Patents

A patent is the grant by a sovereign government of some privilege or authority, typically the exclusive right to make, use, or sell, with respect to an invention (*i.e.*, to exclude others from making, using, or selling the invention). Patents are territorial in nature; they are enforceable only within the territory of the government granting the patent. Typically, patents are granted on a country by

> **Patent**
> The grant of an exclusive right by a sovereign government.

country basis. Various international conventions and treaties, however, accord varying rights in the respective signatory countries to an applicant for a patent in any one of the signatory countries. For example, the International Convention for the Protection of Intellectual Property (Paris Convention) permits the applicant for a patent in one member country to file an application within any other member country within twelve months of the date of the original filing (or within six months of filing for a design patent) and thereby obtain the priority of the original filing date with respect to the subsequent filing. The Patent Cooperation Treaty (PCT) permits a single application to be filed in a designated receiving office and provides for an international search. The application is then forwarded to respective designated individual countries and is processed according to that country's procedures and laws. The European Patent Convention (EPC) established the European Patent Office (EPO) and permits a single application to be filed in the EPO, designating various member countries (limited to European countries) where the patent will apply. The application is examined by the EPO, and ultimately granted or refused in accordance with the law of the treaty. The rights and enforcement of the European patent in the various designated countries are governed by the laws of each individual country, but the validity is governed by the law of the treaty. The patents of the various countries differ widely in scope and effect.

> Patents are typically enforceable only within the territory of the government granting the patent.

Utility Model (Petty Patent)

Some countries grant "petty patents" (sometimes referred to as utility models) on functional elements of a product or process of minor importance, which may not meet minimum requirements for a patent. There is no provision for utility models in the United States.

Copyrights

A copyright is a statutory right provided to the author of a literary or artistic work. The scope and effect of a copyright varies from country to country. However, a number of international conventions and treaties pertain to copyrights, most notably the Pan American Convention of Literary and Artistic Property (Buenos Aires Convention) (subscribed to by numerous countries in the

> A copyright prevents unauthorized copying of works of authorship.

Western hemisphere), the Berne Convention, and the Universal Copyright Convention. In general, a copyright precludes unauthorized copying of artistic or literary aspects of the copyrighted work.

Mask Works

A mask work is a "series of related images, however fixed or enclosed" that represent three dimensional patterns in the layers of a semiconductor chip. The Semiconductor Chip Protection Act has created a statutory protection in the United States for mask works (basically a registration system that incorporates "not commonplace" threshold). Registration precludes the reproduction, importation, or distribution of chips embodying a registered mask work. In essence, registration prevents the use of reproductions of mask works in the manufacture of competing chips. Similar protection has been implemented in a number of other countries.

Trademarks, Reputation, and Goodwill

A trademark (or service mark) is a word or symbol used to distinguish goods or services of one company from those of another. The mark identifies the source of the product or service and, in effect, connects the goodwill and reputation of the company to its products and services.

Under the laws of most countries, a competitor is prevented from capitalizing on a company's reputation and goodwill by using the company's mark (or a similar mark) and attempting to pass off its goods as those made or sponsored by the company. In this way, a trademark protects the market value of the company's reputation and goodwill, and protects investments in advertising and other promotional activities used to develop goodwill.

A **"Trademark"** identifies the source of a product or service.

In some countries, exclusive rights to use a trademark in a given geographical market can be acquired without registering the mark with the government. (In the United States rights can be established by being the first to actually or constructively use the mark. Federal registration can constitute constructive use, effectively expand the geographic scope of the rights, and provide additional remedies.) Other countries, however, require registration and in some cases, various other formalities, as a prerequisite to any exclusive right in the trademark. In fact, a few countries require that a mark be registered with the government before it is used in that country.

Character Trademarks and Sponsorship

Sometimes a product is associated with or sponsored by a celebrity, such as a famous actor or athlete, or a character such as Mickey Mouse, Snoopy, or Indiana Jones. The manifestation of this association, or sponsorship, is actually a form of trademark, sometimes referred to as a character or personality trademark. Some states have also enacted additional statutes specifically directed to the use of a personality's image or voice. A character or celebrity name cannot be associated with a product without permission of the celebrity or owner of the character.

Trade Dress

Trade dress, in general terms, is the appearance and packaging of a product. Where trade dress is sufficiently distinctive, and begins to identify the source, origin, or sponsorship of a product, it can, under the laws of some countries, take on trademark significance and be protected as such.

The Basic Protection Mechanisms

There are five basic legal mechanisms for protecting rights in intellectual property: trade secret protection, patent protection, copyright protection, mask work protection, and trademark protection. Trade secret protection, as the name implies, entails keeping technology secret to prevent the competition from copying the technology. Patent protection is available for inventive concepts embodied in a product, and prevents others from making, using, or selling any product embodying the patented concepts. Copyright protection is available for the form of expression of an idea (as opposed to the idea itself). "Mask work" protection is available for works embodied in semiconductor chips (masks) and prevents others from reproducing, importing, or distributing chips embodying the work. Trademark protection prevents the competition from attempting to trade on a company's reputation.

Protection Mechanisms

- Trade Secret
- Patent
- Copyright
- Mask Work
- Trademark

There are many different aspects of a product embodying technology. For example, with respect to a microprocessor-based product, there are system, component, hardware, and software aspects of the product. The software itself has many aspects: functionality (what the software does), the context of the software in the overall system, the software architecture, algorithms and implementation techniques employed in the software, the code implementing the software, databases operated upon by the software, and documentation. Each of the different aspects

Aspects of a Product

- Functions Performed
- System Context
- Modularity
- Hardware: Overall System/Components
- Software: Architecture/Algorithms/Code
- Mask Works
- Documentation
- Design – Appearance
- Packaging/Trademarks

may be valuable and worthy of protection in its own right.

Each protection mechanism has distinct advantages and disadvantages and provides a varying scope of protection as applied to the different aspects of a product. Combinations of different types of protection can be used to protect different aspects of a product. The particular approach to protecting a given product must be tailored to the specific characteristics and form of the product, and the particular marketing approach and distribution scheme adopted for the product.

The principles discussed below are generally applicable. However, special considerations which arise when a software, firmware, or semiconductor chip product is at issue will also be discussed.

Trade Secret Protection

Any proprietary information not in the public domain can be a "trade secret." Maintaining technology as a "trade secret" protects the technology in the sense that, if the competition doesn't know about the technology, it cannot copy it.

In the United States, trade secret rights that are affirmatively enforceable against others are provided under the laws of the various individual states. Unlike patents, copyrights, mask works, and trademarks there is no federal law directly pertaining to trade secret protection. Accordingly, trade secret rights tend to vary from state to state. However, the existence of the federal patent and copyright statutes has been found to "preempt" the states from enacting statutes that overlap or conflict with the federal law.[2] This has tended to force state trade secret statutes to require the "classical" common law elements for trade secret protection and effectively engendered some commonality in the state laws. Historically, state trade secret laws have differed primarily with respect to treatment of non-technological information, e.g., customer lists, and the extent to which the subject matter at issue had to be unknown to others in order to qualify for the protection. More recently, widespread acceptance of a model trade secret statute, the Uniform

> In the U.S., trade secret rights are governed by the laws of the individual states.

---

[2] See *Bonito Boats, Inc. v. Thunder Craft Boats*, 489 U.S. 141, 152 (1989); *Sears, Roebuck & Co. v. Stiffel Co.*, 376 U.S. 225 (1964); *Compco Corp. v. DayBrite Lighting Inc.*, 376 U.S. 234 (1964); *Roboserve Ltd. v. Tom's Foods Inc.*, 20 U.S.P.Q.2d 1321 (11th Cir. 1991); *Gates Rubber Co. v. Bando American Inc.*, 798 F. Supp. 1489 (D. Colo. 1992); *Cuisinarts Corp. v. Appliance Science Corp.*, 21 U.S. P.Q.2d 1318 (D. Conn. 1991); *Darling v. Standard Alaska Products Co.*, 20 U.S.P.Q.2d 1688, 1691 (Alaska 1991); see also *infra* note 6.

Trade Secrets Act, has brought an additional element of consistency to the trade secret laws of the various states. Some form of the Uniform Trade Secrets Act has presently been adopted in 36 states and the District of Columbia.[3]

In essentially every jurisdiction, however, in order to qualify for the protection, the subject matter of the trade secret right must meet certain prerequisites: it must be confidential (not generally known or readily ascertainable from publicly available information); it must be subject to reasonable efforts to maintain its secrecy (*e.g.*, restricted access, disclosed only under confidentiality agreements, etc.); and it must derive some value from being kept secret.

Scope of Protection

Maintaining technology as a trade secret can protect the technology for a potentially infinite period. The technology is "protected" as long as it is not in the public domain.

> **Trade Secrets Status Cannot Protect Against:**
> - Independent Development
> - Reverse Engineering
> - Use by Innocent Third-Party Recipients

However, a trade secret can be very fragile. Once a trade secret becomes generally known, irrespective of how it becomes known, as a practical matter, trade secret protection is lost. The primary disadvantage of trade secret protection is that absolutely no protection whatsoever is provided against another party independently developing the technology. Moreover, it is conceivable that the second party could obtain a patent on the technology, foreclosing further use of the technology by the first party.

> **An aspect of a product cannot be a trade secret if it is ascertainable from information available to the public.**

It should also be appreciated that some types of technology are totally unsuited for maintaining as a trade secret. Any technology embodied in a product that is sold to the public and can be reverse engineered simply cannot effectively be maintained as a trade secret. *In general, absent an express or implied contractual obligation, a third party is at liberty to use and copy any unpatented, uncopyrighted technology that comes into its possession legally, as long as there is no likelihood that the public would be deceived or confused as to the source of a product.*

---

[3] These states are: Alabama, Alaska, Arizona, Arkansas, California, Colorado, Connecticut, Delaware, Florida, Hawaii, Idaho, Illinois, Indiana, Iowa, Kansas, Kentucky, Louisiana, Maine, Maryland, Minnesota, Mississippi, Montana, Nebraska, Nevada, New Hampshire, New Mexico, North Dakota, Oklahoma, Oregon, Rhode Island, South Dakota, Utah, Virginia, Washington, West Virginia, and Wisconsin.

Procedure for Maintaining a Trade Secret

The procedure for maintaining a trade secret is relatively simple. All technology considered proprietary should be clearly defined as such. As a basic proposition, all printouts, flow charts, schematics, layouts, blueprints, technical data, test results, etc., that contain confidential information should be marked with a proprietary legend.

It is important, however, that a company not be overzealous in categorizing information as confidential, or in the use of nondisclosure and non-compete agreements. Indiscriminate use of proprietary legends can dilute the significance of the legend when used on things that are, in fact, confidential. It can also cause evidentiary problems. Consider the situation of the company that marked a widely distributed manual "Confidential," then years later must prove that a competitor had access to the manual.

> This document comprises confidential information proprietary to X-Corp. This document may not be copied, nor the information herein used, published, or disclosed to others without prior express written authorization of X-Corp.

Tight security should be maintained, and entry and view into the area in which the trade secret is practiced or kept must be restricted. Access to and knowledge of the trade secret should be permitted only on a need-to-know basis. Records should be kept as to all persons given access to any portion of the trade secret. All copies of printouts should be accounted for. For example, it is difficult to assert that a program is a valuable trade secret when it can be shown that the programmer's children took printouts to school to use as scratch paper. Ideally, except for an archive printout of each version of the program, all printouts of trade secret programs and data should be destroyed (*e.g.*, shredded, incinerated, etc.).

Confidentiality agreements should be executed with all parties who are given access to any part of the trade secret technology. In this regard, it is especially important for a company to be sure that any potential customer, vendor or contractor who is permitted access to any aspect of the proprietary technology is required to sign a confidentiality agreement. Moreover, each principal and/or

To Maintain a Trade Secret:
- Use Proprietary Legend on All Documents
- Restrict Access
- Obtain Written Confidentiality Agreements

employee of the company who has access to any aspect of the technology should sign an appropriate employee's invention and confidentiality agreement. Generally, such agreements should be entered into with employees at or prior to hiring the employee. While not necessary in all states,[4] if the individual entering into the agreement is already an employee, it is prudent to give some additional form of consideration (money, promotion, or the like) for signing the agreement. It also may be prudent for a company to adopt a policy of interviewing all exiting employees, to remind them of the confidentiality agreement.

Absent some express or implied contractual obligation to the contrary, a party is under no obligation to maintain information received or obtained in confidence. While an obligation can often be implied as a matter of law or from the surrounding circumstances, a maxim of general applicability that is particularly apropos to trade secrets is: "a verbal agreement is not worth the paper it's written on."

If X-Corp., in Example 5 at the beginning of the handbook, had not divulged the X-Corp. technique until after obtaining a confidentiality agreement from the customer, the customer could possibly have been prevented from disclosing the X-Corp. program to the competition, or made liable for the damage resulting from the disclosure. However, as a practical matter, even if the customer disclosed the program to the competition in violation of an express confidentiality agreement, under many circumstances, it would be impossible to prevent the competition from using the technique after the disclosure.

In some instances, where employees have access to trade secret information and leave the company to take a similar position with a competitor, disclosure or use of the former employer's confidential information may be inevitable, notwithstanding any agreement to the contrary. Where this is the case, a non-competition agreement with the employee should be considered as a mechanism for

Non-competition agreements are strictly construed by the courts.

ensuring the confidential information is not disclosed. However, such agreements are disfavored and strictly construed by the courts. To ensure enforceability, the non-competition agreement should be carefully crafted so that geographic scope, duration, and scope of prohibited employment are restricted to the minimum nec-

---

[4] For example, in Arizona, continued employment is presently sufficient consideration for an employee to enter into such an agreement.

essary to protect the proprietary rights of the former employer; if any of those aspects of the agreement are deemed to be overly broad or over-reaching, a court is likely to find the agreement unenforceable.[5] For example, a non-competition agreement that precludes employment by a competitor irrespective of capacity (*e.g.*, that would preclude a former employee from taking a position as the janitor for a competitor) would likely be deemed overly broad, and hence unenforceable by the courts. The same is true for a non-competition provision of infinite duration. The provision of (or failure to provide) special compensation to the employee for accepting the non-competition obligation may also be a factor in the enforceability of the agreement.

Non-competition agreements should be used judiciously. Use of non-competition agreements with employees that do not have access to confidential information tends to detract from the viability of non-competition agreements in situations where a non-competition agreement may be the only effective mechanism for preventing disclosure or use of confidential information.

Exploiting Trade Secrets

Trade secrets can be exploited through a licensing program. Basically, a third party is permitted to use the trade secret under a license agreement that expressly obligates the third party not to disclose the trade secret and to take various precautions to ensure that the trade secret is not inadvertently disclosed to others. The licensing agreement should be very explicit as to exactly what information is provided to the licensee. However, as a practical matter, it is often difficult to police and enforce trade secret licenses, particularly when there are a substantial number of licensees. Licensing agreements will be more fully discussed in the section titled "Overview and Comparison of Agreements Affecting Intellectual Property Rights and Liabilities" later in this handbook.

Special Considerations with Respect to Software Developments

Trade secret protection for software that is distributed to others (distributed software) is typically effected by licensing others to use the software and/or through various technological mechanisms built into the program that tend to prevent copying.

Technological mechanisms such as encryption, nonstandard formats, a requirement

> Technological mechanisms are sometimes used to restrict access to confidential software.

---

[5] *See, e.g., Scott v. Snelling & Snelling, Inc.*, 732 F. Supp. 1034, 1043 (N.D. Cal. 1990); *Telxon Corp. v. Hoffman*, 13 U.S.P.Q.2d 1577 (N.D. Ill. 1989); *Cambridge Filter Corp. v. International Filter Co.*, 548 F. Supp. 1301 (D. Nev. 1982); *Al S. Chomers v. Continental Aviation & Engineering Corp.*, 255 F. Supp. 645 (E.D. Mich. 1966); *America Broadcasting Companies, Inc. v. Wolf*, 438 N.Y.S.2d 482, 420 N.E. 2d 363 (Ct. App. 1981).

for special interface hardware or, in the case of firmware, encapsulation and/or nonstandard packaging or pinspacing are often used in an attempt to prevent copying. Other security mechanisms are typically used in conjunction with a license, such as techniques for identifying the source of unauthorized copies of a program. For example, a different serial number or other identification is often included in the body of each copy of the program to help identify the source of unauthorized copies. A program may also be "keyed" to a particular hardware system, or include encrypted destruct mechanisms that erase or disable the program, unless periodically "defused" or reset by the licensor. However, potentially serious product liability problems are inherent in the use of some types of physical security mechanisms. Reliability is a major concern. Any physical security mechanism must be capable of reliably discriminating between authorized and unauthorized uses. The failure of a security mechanism, which prevents someone rightfully in possession of a software product from using it, or which destroys a rightful user's database, may result in large damage claims.

A typical software license contains an acknowledgement of the secret or confidential nature of the software and requires the licensee to maintain the software in confidence. For example, the licensee agrees not to show or provide the software to anyone outside of the licensed company without the permission of the licensor. The license often also contains provisions restricting the use of the licensed software, for example, to a designated central processing unit (CPU), or to "internal use only." Under a typical license, the software remains the property of the licensor and the licensor has the right to terminate the license and demand the return of the licensed software if the licensee breaches the license agreement. The license also typically includes "Warranty" or "Warranty Disclaimer" provisions, precisely defining the obligations and liability of the licensor if the program does not operate as expected. The programmer/licensor generally attempts to disclaim all warranties (and thus all liability) including warranties of "merchantability" and "fitness for a particular purpose" often implied by law. From the perspective of the licensee, however, it is desirable to obtain a warranty that the program will operate in the manner represented, *e.g.*, as described in the user's manual.

> **Main Elements of a Typical Software (Trade Secret) License**
>
> - Identity of Parties
> - Identity of Licensed Software
> - Acknowledgment of Proprietary Rights
> - Obligation of Confidentiality
> - Conditions and Limits on Use
> - Limitations on Activities
> - Define/Limit Warranties and Remedies
> - Royalties and Reporting

Trade secret protection of software has a distinct advantage in that, through a license, items that are not necessarily patentable or copyrightable can be protected. However, trade secret protection of a distributed product has the practical disadvantage in that the requisite steps for maintaining secrecy of the product can present a formidable administrative burden. In fact, with respect to very high volume products, such as those relating to personal computers, it is questionable whether any form of licensing would be practicable. The administration of a licensing program requires each "purchaser" of the item to sign a license agreement. Where high volume products are involved, administration can be prohibitively expensive. Often a license is included in the body or packaging of the software product, with a notice on the packaging to the effect that the purchaser agrees to the terms of the license by virtue of opening the package. However, reservations as to the validity of such a "package" license have been expressed, and it is questionable that a true trade secret license exists in such a situation. It can also be argued that sufficient steps have not been taken to preserve the trade secret, thereby forfeiting trade secret status. In this regard, an issue often arises as to how widely a software product can be licensed before the trade secret is lost. That is, how many people can be told a "secret" before it is no longer a secret? Can a product be considered a trade secret when almost everyone who would be interested knows or has access to the secret? These are questions of fact, and must be determined on a case-by-case basis.

Further, an issue has arisen in the courts as to whether it is now even possible to protect software as a trade secret if software is also protectable by copyright. Under the Constitutional "Preemption Doctrine," when a federal statute is applicable in a given area, the states are precluded from also having statutes in respect of that area — the state law is "preempted" by the federal law. It has been argued that, since software may be protected under the federal copyright statute, state trade secret law is preempted. The courts have dealt with the "preemption" issue in a variety of ways.[6] The trend, however, appears to be against finding a state trade secret law preempted as it applies to software, so long as some element is required in addition to the requisite elements for a copyright infringement.[7]

---

[6] *See, e.g., Technicon Medical Information Sys. Corp. v. Green Bay Packaging, Inc.* 687 F.2d 1032, 215 U.S.P.Q. 1001 (7th Cir. 1982); *Gates Rubber Co. v. Bando American Inc.*, 798 F. Supp. 1499 (D. Colo. 1992); *Warrington Assoc., Inc. v. Real-Time Eng'g Sys., Inc.*, 522 F. Supp. 367, 216 U.S.P.Q. 1024 (N.D. Ill. 1981); *Avdo Corp. v. Precision Air Parts, Inc.*, 210 U.S.P.Q. 894 (M.D. Ala. 1980); *Synercom Technology, Inc. v. University Computing Co.*, 474 F. Supp. 37, 204 U.S.P.Q. 29 (N.D. Tex. 1979); *M. Bryce & Assoc., Inc. v. Gladstone*, 107 Wis.2d 241, 319 N.W.2d 907, 215 U.S.P.Q. 81 (App. 1982).

[7] *See, e.g., Gates Rubber Co. v. Bando American, Inc.* 798 F. Supp. at 1522.

Patent Protection

Patent protection potentially excludes others from making, using, or selling any product which incorporates the central idea or concept of an invention. Obtaining one or more patents on the inventive portions of a product can provide the broadest scope of legal protection. Conversely, as a basic proposition, absent some contractual obligation or likelihood of confusion as to source, anyone can make, use, or sell unpatented products.

Utility Patent Protection

In most countries, other than the United States, a patent grant originated as a gift or favor from the sovereign. In fact, many of the early "patents" granted in Europe had nothing to do with invention; they related to exclusive trading rights within a geographic region or to ownership of land. So, in part because of the differing origins, the philosophy of the United States and the various foreign systems are subtly different. This tends to be reflected in subtle (and not so subtle) differences between the patent laws of the United States and other countries.

The basis for the patent system in the United States is the federal Constitution. Article I, Section VIII of the Constitution provides: "The Congress shall have the power . . . to promote the progress of science and useful arts, by securing for a limited time to authors and inventors the exclusive right to their respective writings and discoveries." Congress then had to develop some system for inducing an "inventor" to make the necessary investment of time and money in research, while at the same time ensuring that the work of the inventor would ultimately become available to the public. The result is the patent system.

> **Patent *Quid Pro Quo***
>
> In return for teaching the public how to make and use the invention, the inventor is given the exclusive right to make, use, and sell the invention for a period of time.

Thus, in a nutshell, a patent in the United States is a *"quid pro quo"* ("give and take") agreement between an inventor and the government. The inventor teaches the public, in enough detail to enable a person "of ordinary skill" in the field of the invention (the average engineer, technician, scientist, or worker in the particular area of technology of the invention), how to make and use the invention without undue experimentation. In return, the inventor is given the right to exclude the public from making, using, or selling the invention for a period of up to 17 years from the date that the patent is granted.

The inventor's investment is protected by the award of "exclusive rights" to the invention. In return, the public is provided with a teaching of how to use the invention, and while the public cannot make, use, or sell the invention during the 17-year period (unless licensed by the patent owner), further research can begin at the point where the invention left off. In addition, after the patent lapses, the public is free to use the invention. In this way, the patent system provides both protection to the inventor and a very real benefit to the public.

> The basis of the patent and copyright law in the United States is the federal constitution.

Because of this *quid pro quo* between the inventor and the government, a patent grant is divided into two major parts: the written description, which includes a detailed description of the invention; and the claims, which define the rights of the inventor. This will be discussed in more detail later in the handbook.

Exclusive Right

> Obtaining a patent does not ensure the ability to use the invention; use of a patented invention may still infringe another patent.

In order to promote improvements on inventions by providing patent protection for the improvements without degrading the protection provided for basic inventions, a patent provides an *"exclusive"* (exclusionary) right to the inventor. That is, the patentee has the right to exclude others from practicing the invention. *However, the patentee does not necessarily have the right to practice his invention himself.*[8]

---

[8] *Vaupel Textilmaschinen RG v. Meccanica Euro Italia S.P.A.*, 944 F.2d 870 (Fed. Cir. 1991).

An unauthorized item infringes a patent if it includes elements corresponding to each and every element in any claim in the patent. It is irrelevant that the item includes additional elements, even if the additional elements (or combination) is patentable in their own right.

> A device infringes a patent if it includes elements corresponding to each and every element of a patent claim.

The classic example illustrating the "exclusive" nature of patent protection is that of the "stool" versus the "chair." Assume that Inventor A has just invented and obtained patent protection on the "stool": a seat and a support structure for maintaining the seat at a predetermined level from the ground. Inventor B thereafter purchases a stool and finds that he has difficulties remaining seated — every time he leans back, he falls off! Ultimately, Inventor B develops a back for his stool and invents the "chair." Inventor B then obtains patent protection on the "chair": a seat, a support structure for maintaining the seat at a predetermined level from the ground, and a back extending above the seat.

Both Inventor A and Inventor B have patents. However, notwithstanding the addition of the "back," Inventor B's "chair" still includes elements corresponding to each and every element of Inventor A's basic patent on the "stool." Similarly, while Inventor A is free to make, use and sell his "stool" (assuming that no other patents cover his stool structure), he cannot put a back on his "stool" without infringing Inventor B's patent on the "chair."

How does this promote the advance of technology? As a practical matter, the result is that Inventors A and B each obtain licenses from the other under the respective patents, and, where before there was only one "stool" manufacturer, there are suddenly two "chair" manufacturers.

This example is overly simplistic, and it has obviously been quite some time since the stool or chair *per se* have been patentable inventions. However, the example does illustrate the "exclusive" nature of patent protection.

The "exclusive" nature of the patent grant is of consequence with respect to the procedures that should be followed by a company before introducing a new product. The issue of whether any aspect of the product is patentable is entirely different and distinct from the issue of whether the product infringes any patent held by another. Before introducing a new product both of these issues should be studied thoroughly.

Ownership of a Patent

As a basic proposition, absent some express or implied contractual agreement to the contrary, the ownership of a patent is in the inventor. Where there are joint inventors, each owns an equal undivided interest in the whole of the patent. Absent an agreement to the contrary, all joint inventors are entitled to make, use, and sell (and license others to make, use, and sell) the invention, without accounting to the other co-inventors.[9]

> Absent an express or implied agreement, a patent is owned by the inventor.

Under certain circumstances, rights in an invention are held by an employer. For example, where an employee is specifically hired to develop a particular product, there is an implied agreement that the employer will own all rights to that product. Similarly, where an invention is made on company time and/or using company facilities, the company may acquire "shop rights" (in essence a royalty free license to use) to the invention.[10] However, disputes often arise as to whether an employee was hired to make a given invention (was the invention within the scope of employment?) or whether the employer consented to the use of facilities or otherwise released its rights in a development. Accordingly, companies typically require each employee to execute an "employee's invention agreement" as a condition of employment—obligating the employee to assign all rights in inventions to the company. However, a number of states[11] have enacted statutes which limit the permissible scope of such agreements, and place certain restrictions on an employer's ability to require employees to assign all inventions made during the term of their employment. These statutes, in effect, preclude an employer from compelling assignments of inventions which fall outside of the field of the company business, were developed by the employee outside of their scope of employment, and were developed without the use of company time or resources.

Recording of Assignments, Grants, and Conveyances

Any transfer of ownership (assignment) of a patent must be in writing. It must also be recorded with the U.S. Patent and Trademark Office (PTO) in order to be effective against any subsequent purchaser for value without knowledge.[12] Security interests in patents must also be recorded with the PTO in order to be effective against any subsequent purchaser that "pays" value for the security interest (*i.e.*,

---

[9] *See* 35 U.S.C. §262; *Willingham v. Star Cutter Co.*, 555 F.2d 1340, 1344 (6th Cir. 1977); *Lemelson v. Synergistics Res. Co.*, 669 F. Supp. 642, 645 (S.D. N.Y. 1987).
[10] *See United States v. Dubliler Condenser Corp.*, 289 U.S. 178 (1938); *Marshall v. Colgate Palmolive-Peet Co.*, 175 F.2d 215 (3d Cir. 1949); *Wellington Print Works v. Magid*, 242 F. Supp. 614 (E.D. Pa. 1965); *Simms v. Mac Truck Corp.*, 488 F. Supp. 592 (E.D. Pa. 1980).
[11] For example, Minnesota, Washington, California, Utah, North Carolina, and Illinois.
[12] 35 U.S.C. §261.

> Any transfer of ownership must be recorded in the PTO.

the security interest is not a gift) and without knowledge of the prior purchase.

It may also be prudent to file financing statements with respect to the security interest under the Uniform Commercial Code (UCC).[13] The UCC treats patents (as well as the other forms of intellectual property) as "general intangibles." Security interests in general intangibles are perfected by filing a financing statement with a state government agency (typically the Secretary of State). The holder of a perfected UCC security interest has priority over unperfected security interests, subsequent purchasers, and holders of subsequently perfected security interests. The holder of a perfected security interest has priority over most lien creditors, and over the rights of the trustee or debtor-in-possession in bankruptcy.

Patentable Subject Matter; Applicability to Software Inventions

Patent protection is available for "any new and useful process, machine, manufacture or composition of matter, or any new and useful improvement thereof."[14] An invention in any one of those categories is generally patentable if it is neither "anticipated" by (identical to)[15] nor "obvious"[16] in view of previous technology. As a general proposition, there is no question that electronic or mechanical apparatus, electronic systems, and components are patentable subject matter.

> **Patentable?**
> - "Any new and useful process, machine, manufacture or composition of matter or any new and useful improvement thereof"
> - Novel
> - Not Obvious

Historically, however, there has been a great deal of controversy in the courts as to whether software and firmware developments come within any of the categories specified by the statute. It is now clear, however, that the majority of software and firmware inventions are, in fact, patentable subject matter.

---

[13] While the federal statutes make recording with the PTO requisite, and may make a UCC filing unnecessary, it is clearly permissible. It is recommended that mortgages, collateral assignments, and other security interests be recorded both in the PTO and perfected under the UCC.
[14] 35 U.S.C. §101.
[15] 35 U.S.C. §102.
[16] 35 U.S.C. §103.

The courts have determined that certain things are definitely outside the categories of patentable subject matter—

- **Mere printed matter**

    One cannot patent a set of words. (However, patent protection might be available for embodiments of the *concept* described by the words or the way paper is folded or perforated relative to printed matter.[17])

- **Methods of doing business**

    Patent protection is not available, for example, for an advertising gimmick, such as the idea of "a two-for-one sale."

- **Things unaltered from a natural state**

    For example, a rock taken unaltered from the earth is not, *per se*, patentable. (However, a given *method of using* the rock might be patentable.)

- **Abstract scientific principles**

    Abstract principles, divorced from any physical structure (*e.g.*, laws of nature) are not, *per se*, patentable. For example, Newton could not have patented "gravity."

How do software inventions fit into a permissible category? Since mere printed matter is not patentable, software documentation describing a program is not, in itself, patentable. The issue, however, is whether the underlying idea of the program is patentable as a "new and useful process." If so, execution of a patented program in a machine or computer, or sale of a disc or ROM containing the program, would be an infringement of the patent.

The controversy over the availability of patent protection for computer programs arose because, at one time, some courts equated computer programs with mathematical algorithms. Mathematical algorithms, in the abstract, are considered to be mere manifestations of scientific principles. Consider, for example, the equation $E = mc^2$. The equation is, in effect, an abstract scientific principle.

---

[17] See U.S. Patent No. 4,614,364 issued September 30, 1986, relating to an advertising insert.

However, the courts have now recognized that a computer program is not necessarily equivalent to a mathematical algorithm or law of nature. Two cases related to the patentability of software[18] and firmware[19] were decided by the Supreme Court in 1981. *In essence, the Supreme Court held that the fact that the inventive concept of an otherwise patentable invention resides in a programmed computer or in firmware does not make the invention unpatentable.* The Supreme Court did not, however, specifically reach the issue of whether software or firmware, outside of the context of a hardware system or process, is patentable subject matter, and the Supreme Court cases did not in themselves end the controversy.

In October of 1982, the Court of Appeals for the Federal Circuit (CAFC), was created with jurisdiction over all appeals from the U.S. district courts relating to patent matters (and, in most cases, appeals from the Patent and Trademark Office decisions). The CAFC was formed by combining the Court of Customs and Patent Appeals (CCPA) and the U.S. Court of Claims, and has expressly adopted the body of law developed earlier by the CCPA and Court of Claims.[20] This is particularly significant because it is likely that the Supreme Court will defer to the CAFC's expertise in patent and other technological matters and, therefore, as a practical matter, the ultimate "law" on the patentability of software will be determined by the CAFC. The CCPA (and thus the CAFC) had for a number of years, recognized that "computer program" and "mathematical algorithm" are not synonymous, and considers only mathematical algorithms to be unpatentable subject matter. In this regard, the CCPA has adopted a two-part test to determine whether a given patent claim covers patentable subject matter. The CCPA has construed the Supreme Court cases to support this two-part test.

Under the CCPA test, the claim is first analyzed to see if a mathematical algorithm (defined as a "procedure for solving a given type of mathematical problem") is directly or indirectly recited. If not, the claim is directed to patentable subject matter. If a mathematical algorithm is found, the claim as a whole is then further analyzed to determine whether the algorithm is "applied in any manner to physical elements or process steps." If the physical elements or process steps are present, the claim "passes muster" under the patent statute.[21]

---

[18] *Diamond v. Diehr,* 450 U.S. 175, 101 S. Ct. 1048 (1981).
[19] *Diamond v. Bradley,* 450 U.S. 381, 101 S. Ct. 1495 (1981).
[20] *South Corp. & Seal Fleet, Inc. v. United States,* 690 F.2d 1368 (Fed. Cir. 1982).
[21] *In re Freeman,* 573 F.2d 1237, 197 U.S.P.Q. 464 (C.C.P.A. 1978), *as modified by In re Walter,* 618 F.2d 758 (C.C.P.A. 1980); *see also In re Meyer,* 688 F.2d 789 (C.C.P.A. 1982); *In re Maucorps,* 609 F.2d 481 (C.C.P.A. 1979); *In re Gelnovatch,* 594 F.2d 32 (C.C.P.A. 1979); *In re Johnson,* 589 F.2d 1070 (C.C.P.A. 1978); *In re Sarkar,* 588 F.2d 1330 (C.C.P.A. 1978); *In re Waldbaum,* 559 F.2d 611 (C.C.P.A. 1977); *In re Deutsch,* 553 F.2d 689 (C.C.P.A. 1977); *In re Chetfield,* 545 F.2d 152 (C.C.P.A. 1976); *cert denied,* 434 U.S. 875 (1977).

In applying the first part of the two-part test to a compiler program, the CCPA has stated:

> It is [a mathematical] algorithm that constitutes nonstatutory subject matter, and this court has consistently rejected attempts to enlarge the "mathematical algorithm" exception to the definition of patentable subject matter in section 101 to include nonmathematical algorithms.[22]

The court held that patent protection was available for the compiler program:

> Appellants' method claims are directed to executing programs in a computer. The method operates on any program and any formula which may be input, regardless of mathematical content. That a computer controlled according to the invention is capable of handling mathematics is irrelevant to the question of whether a mathematical algorithm is recited by the claims.[23]

The court found that steps of examining, compiling, storing, and executing used to describe the program do not involve any mathematical algorithm, and thus define patentable subject matter. Thus, patent protection is available for computer programs, *per se*, except perhaps in the case of pure "number cruncher" type programs where the inventive concept is a particular mathematical formula implemented by the program (as opposed to the particular manner in which the mathematical formula is implemented by the program).

Moreover, under the CCPA test, even where a mathematical algorithm is involved, patent protection may still be possible so long as the algorithm is "applied in any manner" to physical elements or process steps.[24] Thus, patent protection may be available for even a "number cruncher" program, when used in a physical system or apparatus. Of course, in practice, the majority of number cruncher programs either are used in conjunction with physical systems or processes, and are therefore protectable, or are valuable because of some economy in memory or execution time provided by the implementation of a formula rather than the formula itself. It is the feature that saves memory or time that is to be protected — not the formula — and the feature, defined in terms of the steps of examining, storing, executing, etc., is patentable subject matter.

In more recent cases, the CAFC has confirmed the patentability of processes or methods performed by a computer in accordance with a program.[25]

---

[22] *In re Pardo and Landau*, 684 F.2d 912, 214 U.S.P.Q. 673, 676 (C.C.P.A. 1982).
[23] *Id.* at 677.
[24] *In re Taner*, 681 F.2d 787, 214 U.S.P.Q. 678 (C.C.P.A. 1982); In re Abele, 684 F.2d 902, 214 U.S.P.Q. 682 (C.C.P.A. 1982).
[25] *In re Alappat*, ___ F.2d ___, 31 U.S.P.Q.2d 1545 (Fed. Cir. 1994); *Arrhythmia Research Technology v. Corazonix Corp.*, 958 F.2d 1053 (Fed. Cir. 1992); *Atari Games Corp. v. Nintendo of America, Inc.*, 975 F.2d 832 (Fed. Cir. 1992); *In re Iwahashi*, 12 U.S.P.Q.2d 1908 (Fed. Cir. 1989).

In light of the Supreme Court and CAFC decisions, the PTO has adopted the CCPA two-part test for patentable subject matter.[26] However, notwithstanding the subject matter, the manner in which a patent claim is drafted can be determinative.[27]

Patent protection for software has successfully been obtained and exploited. Patents on software inventions are now common.[28] Software patents are held by numerous companies, notably, Allied Corp., Amalgamated Software of North America, American Chemical Society, AT&T Bell Labs, Bachman Infosystems, Becton Dickinson & Co., Bull, Burroughs Corp., Chevron Research Co., Computer Service Co., CSP, Inc., Data General Corp., Delta Telephone Labs, Diamond Shamrock Corp., Digital Equipment Corp., Duquesne Systems, Inc., General Electric, Hitachi, Honeywell, Hughes Aircraft Company, IBM, IO Data Corp., Johns Hopkins University, Measurex Corp., Nippon Denso, Nippon Electric, Nissan Motor Company, Ltd., Perken Elmer Corp., Schlumberger, S&H Computer Systems, Siber-Geigy Corp., Storage Technology Corp., Systems Development Company, Tanavary Timber Co., Tandy Corp., Techtronics, Teknowledge, Inc., Texas Instruments, Toshiba, Unisys Corp., United Technologies Corp., U.S. Army, U.S. Department of Commerce, U.S. NASA, U.S. Navy, U.S. Phillips Corp., Varian Associates, Inc., Volt Delta Resources, Wang Lab, Westinghouse, Xerox, and others, as well as many individuals. Patents on purely software inventions have been upheld by the courts.[29] The author has been involved in obtaining and successfully exploiting patents on various aspects of both compiler-type and applications-type programs, as well as on

Which Aspects of a Software Product are Patentable?

Aspect	Patentable Subject Matter?
Functionality	Yes
System Context	Yes
Architecture	Yes
Algorithims	Two-step test
Implementation	Yes
Code	Typically not
Database	Typically not
Documentation	Typically not

---

[26] *Manual of Patent Examining Procedure* §2100 Fifth Edition, latest revision August 1993; "Patentable Subject Matter, Mathematical Algorithms and Computer Programs," 1106 Off. Gaz. Pat. Office 5 (Sept. 5, 1989); "Notice Interpreting *Iwahashi* (Fed. Cir. 1989)," 1112 Off. Gaz. Pat. Office 18 (Mar. 13, 1990).
[27] *See In re Grams,* 888 F.2d 835 (Fed . Cir. 1989); *Ex parte Akamatsu,* 22 U.S.P.Q.2d 1915, 1918 (PTO Board of Appeals 1992); *Ex parte Logan,* 20 U.S.P.Q.2d 1465 (PTO Board of Appeals 1991); *see also In re Zeltz,* 892 F.2d 319 (Fed. Cir. 1989); *In re Priest,* 582 F.2d 33, 37 (C.C.P.A.1978).
[28] See Patents classified in PTO Class 364 (Electronic Computer and Data Processors), Subclasses 300 (Programming Methods or Procedures), 200 (General Purpose Programmable Digital Computer Systems), and 900 (Miscellaneous Digital Data Processing Systems).
[29] *Paine, Webber, Jackson & Curtis, Inc. v. Merrill Lynch, Pierce, Fenner & Smith, Inc.,* 564 F. Supp. 1358, 218 U.S.P.Q. 212 (D. Del. 1983); *Stac Electronics v. Microsoft Corp.,* Case No. CV 93-0413-ER (BX) (C.D. Cal. 1994).

microprocessor based systems which have an inventive concept embodied primarily in the software or firmware (as opposed to the hardware) of the system.

Statutory Bars

"Novelty" Is Defined By Statute: 35 U.S.C. §102

The patent statute expressly precludes obtaining a patent under certain circumstances. In theory, under specific circumstances set forth in the patent statute, the invention is considered either to have already passed into the public domain, *i.e.*, become public property, or to have already become the property of another and hence not to be patentable. These circumstances are referred to as "statutory bars." These are the pitfalls that so often trip up the unwary. The patent statute regarding "novelty" sets forth the statutory bars.[30] Each of the statutory bars will be discussed individually below.

Prior Public Knowledge

An inventor is not entitled to a patent on an invention if the invention is publicly known before the inventor conceives it. The statute states:

> §102 A person shall be entitled to a patent unless—
> (a) the invention was known or used by others in this country, or patented or described in a printed publication in this or a foreign country, before the invention thereof by the applicant for patent...

This bar has been construed to mean the invention must not have been *publicly* known or used by others in the United States, or patented or described in a *printed* publication anywhere in the world, before the "inventor" *conceived* the invention. In other words, if the public knew about an "invention" before the applicant for a patent conceived the idea, the invention is public property (or already the property of another) and the applicant cannot obtain a patent on it. As will be discussed, secret (non-public) use of the invention *by another* will not necessarily operate as a bar.[31]

---

[30] 35 U.S.C. §102.
[31] *See J.A. LaPorte, Inc. v. Norfolk Dredging Co.*, 787 F.2d 1577 (Fed. Cir. 1986); *W.L.Gore & Associates, Inc. v. Garlock, Inc.*, 721 F.2d 1540 (Fed. Cir. 1983).

Patents that are already issued are proof of that which the public knows at the time of an invention. In this regard, the statute also states:

> §102 A person shall be entitled to a patent unless—
> . . . .
> (e) the invention was described in a patent granted on an application for patent by another filed in the United States before the invention thereof by the applicant for patent, or on an interntional application by another who has fulfilled the requirements of paragraphs (1), (2), and (4) of section 371(c) of this title before the invention thereof by the applicant for patent. . . .

This paragraph of the statute establishes the *filing* date of a patent (the date when the application for the patent was filed) as the date that the patent becomes "prior art." In other words, the patent is considered proof that the invention was known "by others" at least as early as the filing date of the patent (*i.e.*, is either public property or the property of another). Therefore, if a patent describing the invention was filed before the person applying for a patent conceived the invention, it is clear that the invention was "previously known by others," and the later applicant is not entitled to a patent.

> **Statutory Bars: Not New**
> Bar if invention was publicly known by others *before conception* by applicant:
> - Publicly known/used by others in United States
> - Patented or described in printed publication anywhere in world
> - Described in U.S. or PCT patent filed before conception

Premature Disclosure or Sale

The inventor can also lose rights by prematurely disclosing, selling, or using his invention in public. The statute states:

> §102 A person shall be entitled to a patent unless—
> . . . .
> (b) the invention was patented or described in a printed publication in this or a foreign country or in public use or on sale in this country, more than one year prior to the date of the application for patent in the United States. . . .

> **Premature Disclosure or Commercialization Can Create a Bar Subject to a One-Year Grace Period:**
>
> Bar if more than one year before U.S. Application
> - Patented or described in printed publication
> - Publicly used or offered for sale in the U.S.

The so-called "publication," "public use," and "on sale" bars of §102(b) are traps which have caught many an unwary company. For example, in Example 2 at the beginning of the handbook, it was the "public use" and "on sale" bars that precluded Z-Corp. from protecting its R & D investment. There are two reasons for this section of the statute. The first reason is to prevent a patentee from, in effect, extending the term of a patent beyond the statutory limit (17 years) by filing a patent application only after first exploiting the invention until competitive products begin to appear. The second reason is to provide a degree of certainty as to whether or not technology is within the public domain. If technology is available or known to the public for a certain period of time and is not the subject of a patent or patent application, the public should be entitled to assume that the technology is in the public domain. Accordingly, under the statute, if an application is not filed, the technology is deemed to be in the public domain after being available to the public for more than one year. By not seeking a patent until more than one year after introducing the product, Z-Corp., in effect, dedicated its R & D investment to the public.

Patented

The term "patented" in this portion of the statute has been construed to mean that the invention is already "claimed" or "protected" under the laws of the particular country that issued the patent. The effective date of the "patent" is also a function of the particular country. A patent, of course, can also be a printed publication bar, as will be discussed below. It should be noted that it does not matter who the patentee is; depending on timing, the inventor's own prior patents can constitute a bar under this section.

Described in a Printed Publication

To constitute a possible "publication" bar, an item must (1) describe the invention, (2) be "printed," and (3) be "published." In this context "printed" means any visually reproducible form, *i.e.*, printed, xerographic reproductions, microfilm, etc. The requirement for "publication" under the patent statute is very different from publication in the copyright sense. *"Publication" under the patent statute* has come to mean only that the document be accessible to that class of persons concerned with the art to which the document relates and thus most likely to avail themselves of its contents. Factors bearing on whether a document is published under the patent statute include the number of copies made, availability, accessibility, dissemination, and, sometimes, the intent of the author.[32] Depositing copies of an "unpublished work" (in the copyright sense) with the Library of Congress constitutes publication under the patent statute.

A document is published when it actually becomes accessible. For example, a magazine becomes "published" in the patent law sense, not as of the date it is placed in the mail, but rather the date that it reaches its subscribers. The author of the publication is irrelevant. Depending on timing, papers *by the inventor* describing an invention can constitute a bar to a patent on the invention.

Public Use

In the context of the statute, "public use" means used in public, either by a third party or *the inventor himself*. Any use of the invention by the inventor or his company in the ordinary course of business for trade or profit puts the invention in "public use," even if the use itself is secret and the public would have no way of ascertaining the use.[33] For example, if the invention is a new manufacturing technique, sale of products made by that manufacturing technique by the inventor or his company constitutes a public use and may be a bar.

Similarly, any *non-secret* use of the invention by a third party in the ordinary course of business is a potential bar to obtaining the patent. Even if a third party uses the invention in secret, a potential public use bar arises if the invention can be determined by inspection or analysis of a resulting product sold or publicly displayed by the third party. However, if it could not be determined from the product that the invention was used by the third party, the use is not considered "public."[34] For example, if the invention is a manufacturing technique maintained as a "trade secret" by a third party, and one could not analyze the products and "reverse engineer" the manufacturing techniques, it is not considered a public use. Similarly, if the invention is a program or programming technique maintained as a trade secret (even if licensed as such) by a third party, it is not considered a public use. In contrast, however, as noted above, where it is the *inventor* who sells or displays a product made using the manufacturing technique, the sale

---

[32] *See Constant v. Advance Micro Devices, Inc.*, 848 F.2d 1560 (Fed. Cir. 1988); *In re Hall*, 781 F.2d 897 (Fed. Cir. 1986); *Massachusetts Institute of Technology v. A.B. Fortia*, 777 F.2d 1104 (Fed. Cir. 1985); *see also Northern Telcom, Inc. v. Datapoint Corp.*, 908 F.2d 931 (Fed Cir. 1990); *In re Cronyn*, 890 F.2d 1158 (Fed. Cir. 1989); *Preemption Devices, Inc. v. Minnesota Mining & Manufacturing Co.*, 732 F.2d 903 (Fed. Cir. 1984).

[33] *See, e.g., In re Mann*, 861 F.2d 1581 (Fed. Cir. 1988); *Harrington Manufacturing Co. v. Powell Manufacturing Co.*, 815 F.2d 1478 (Fed. Cir. 1986).

[34] *See W.L. Gore & Associates, Inc. v. Garlock, Inc.*, 721 F.2d 1540 (Fed. Cir. 1983); *see also J.A. LaPorte, Inc. v. Norfolk Dredging Co.*, 787 F.2d 1577 (Fed. Cir. 1986).

or display is a potential bar whether or not the manufacturing technique can be reverse engineered.[35]

Most importantly, when an invention is the subject of a showing or demonstration to one or more prospective purchasers or licensees, the demonstration is frequently considered to be a "public use." A "public use" can be avoided in such situations if confidentiality agreements are signed by the persons viewing the demonstration. However, even with confidentiality agreements, the demonstration may constitute a potential "on sale" bar, as will be discussed later.[36]

There is an exception to the "public use" bar for experimental uses under the strict direction and control of the inventor (and/or the inventor's company). In general, to qualify as an experimental use, the subjective intent of the inventor (or the inventor's company) must be to test the invention, rather than a profit motive.[37] There must be direct and continual feedback of the results of the "testing" to the inventor.[38] There should also be as little "publicity" as possible.[39] One must also distinguish an experimental use to test the invention and prove that it works, from market testing designed to determine market acceptance of a product, a regulatory testing procedure, or features not part of the invention claimed.[40]

Whether or not a use is experimental is a very technical (in the legal sense) question, and it is prudent to not have to rely on the experimental use exception. The issue, however, is easily avoided by taking timely actions to protect inventions.

On Sale

In the context of the statute, the term "on sale" is interpreted to mean "offered for sale, or sold." A mere offer to sell or license the invention or a product embodying the invention is a possible bar, even if the offer is never received by a prospective purchaser. Also, a sale or offer to sell need not be "public." Even a "secret sale" (offer to sell or license, under a confidentiality agreement) is a potential bar to

---

[35] *See Kinzenbaw v. Deere & Co.*, 741 F.2d 383 (Fed. Cir. 1984).
[36] *See, e.g., In re Fritch*, 972 F.2d 1260 (Fed. Cir. 1992); *In re Gorman*, 933 F.2d 982 (Fed. Cir. 1991); *Gillette Co. v. S.C. Johnson & Sons, Inc.*, 919 F.2d 720 (Fed. Cir. 1990); *Grain Processing Corp. v American Maize Products Corp.*, 840 F.2d 902 (Fed. Cir. 1988); *Hartness International, Inc. v. Simplimatic Engineering Co.*, 819 F.2d 1100 (Fed. Cir. 1987).
[37] *See LaBounty Manufacturing, Inc. v. ITC*, 958 F.2d 1066 (Fed. Cir. 1992); *Manville Sales Corp. v. Paramount Systems, Inc.*, 917 F.2d 544 (Fed. Cir. 1990); *Grain Processing Corp. v. American Maize Products Corp.*, 840 F.2d 902 (Fed. Cir. 1988); *In re Brigance*, 792 F.2d 1103 (Fed. Cir. 1986).
[38] *See U.S. Environmental Products, Inc. v. Westall*, 911 F.2d 713 (Fed. Cir. 1990); *In re Hamilton*, 882 F.2d 1576 (Fed. Cir. 1989); *Baker Oil Tools, Inc. v. Geo Vann, Inc.*, 828 F.2d 1588 (Fed. Cir. 1987); *Western Marine Electronics, Inc. v. Furuno Electric Co.*, 764 F.2d 840 (Fed. Cir. 1985).
[39] *U.S. Environmental Products, Inc. v. Westall*, 911 F.2d 713 (Fed. Cir. 1990).
[40] *See, e.g., RCA Corp. V. Data General Corp.*, 887 F.2d 1056 (Fed. Cir. 1989); *In re Mann*, 861 F.2d 1581 (Fed. Cir. 1988); *In re Brigance*, 792 F.2d 1103 (Fed. Cir. 1986); *Pennwalt Corp. v. Akzona, Inc.*, 740 F.2d 1573 (Fed. Cir. 1984); *In re Smith*, 714 F.2d 1127 (Fed. Cir. 1983).

obtaining a patent.[41] Advertisements in a trade journal or a direct mailing of brochures typically constitute an offer for sale (as well as a printed publication) that can potentially bar patent protection.

Strict Novelty in Most Foreign Countries

The law in the United States is very strict with regard to publication, on sale, and public use bars. A single publication, sale or public use *more than one year before the patent application is filed in the United States* is deadly. Yet the United States is considered charitable when compared to many of the foreign countries. The United States, in effect, provides an inventor a one-year grace period from the sale, use, or publication in which to legitimately claim his rights. *Most foreign countries, however, do not provide any grace period. Any description of the invention published prior to the filing of a patent application bars the inventor from obtaining patent protection in most foreign countries.*

> **Foreign Rights: No Grace Period**
>
> - Any description of the invention published before filing the application precludes most foreign patent protection.

In this connection, the United States has entered into treaties with most of the technologically developed countries, which give the inventor the benefit in the foreign country of the date that the inventor's U.S. application was filed, as long as a corresponding patent application is filed in the foreign country within a predetermined period. Thus, publications made after filing the U.S. application generally do not prejudice the inventor's rights in those foreign countries. In Example 3 given at the beginning of the handbook, if Dr. A had waited until after a U.S. patent application had been filed before publishing the paper on his devices, Y-Corp. would not have been barred from obtaining protection for the device in Japan and Germany.

It is not always wise, however, to publish a paper on an invention before a patent is actually granted. Patent application files in the United States are maintained in secrecy. If a patent application is filed on a process or programming technique and it is later determined that the program is unpatentable, it may still be possible to maintain the program as a trade secret if there has been no publication in the interim.

---

[41] *See, e.g., J.A. LaPorte, Inc. v. Norfolk Dredging Co.*, 787 F.2d 1577 (Fed. Cir. 1986).

Abandonment

Another way to lose patent rights is through an abandonment. The statute states:

> § 102 A person shall be entitled to a patent unless—
> . . . .
> (c) he has abandoned the invention . . . .

Someone who abandons an invention may not thereafter be entitled to a patent on the invention. For example, assume that a number of years ago, Mr. D had an idea for a new interface circuit, but had come to the conclusion that it was not worth pursuing and put it aside. A number of years after the fact, lo and behold, Mr. D finds out that P Company is about to come out with a line of hardware using precisely the interface circuit that he had conceived years before. Mr. D goes directly to his patent attorney and requests that an application be filed. It is determined that Mr. D, in fact, developed the interface before P Company, and the application could be filed within one year of any "printed publication," "public use," or "on sale" bars. Just the same, Mr. D is barred from obtaining a patent because he had "abandoned" the invention.

"Abandonment" is a matter of the subjective intent of the inventor, as well as the facts surrounding the inventor's activities.[42] However, as a rule of thumb, any time someone "sits on" an invention, doing nothing for more than two years, the person is presumed to have abandoned the invention.

Foreign Patent Applications Can Create a Statutory Bar:

- Premature filing of Foreign Application/Foreign Filing License
- Delayed filing of U.S. Application:
  — Foreign Application filed more than one year before U.S. Application and
  — Foreign Application issues as patent before U.S. Application filed

Corresponding Foreign Patent Applications

An inventor in the United States can lose patent rights in the United States by filing a foreign patent application prematurely. Any time a U.S. company files an application for a patent on an invention in a foreign country prior to, or within six months after, filing an application on the invention in the United States, the company must first obtain a "Foreign Filing License" from the PTO, or a U.S. patent will be barred.[43]

---

[42] *See Paulik v. Rizkalla*, 760 F.2d 1270 (Fed. Cir. 1985).
[43] 35 U.S.C. §§184, 185.

An inventor can also lose patent rights in the United States through delay after filing a patent application on the invention in a foreign country. The statute provides:

> §102 A person shall be entitled to a patent unless—
> . . . .
> (d) the invention was first patented or caused to be patented, or was the subject of an inventor's certificate, by the applicant or his legal representatives or assigns in a foreign country prior to the date of the application for patent in this country on an application for patent or inventor's certificate filed more than twelve months before the filing of the application in the United States. . . .

Under this paragraph of the statute, a bar arises if (1) the inventor or his company or his legal representatives, (2) files an application for a patent on the invention in a foreign country, (3) more than one year before filing an application in the United States, *and* (4) the foreign application issues as a patent prior to the filing of the application in the United States.

Actual Inventor

A U.S. patent on an invention can be obtained only by the actual inventor. This is in contradistinction to most other countries in the world; most other countries permit a patent to be filed in the name of its owner, e.g., employer, rather than in the names of the actual individual inventor(s). This distinction in the United States patent law relates back to the constitutional origins of the U.S. patent system. The Constitution provides that "The Congress shall have power . . . to promote the progress of science and useful arts by securing for limited times to *authors and inventors* the exclusive right to their respective writings and discoveries." Accordingly, the statute provides:

> §102 A person shall be entitled to a patent unless—
> . . . .
> (f) he did not himself invent the subject matter sought to be patented. . . .

In order to obtain a patent, the entity (one or more persons) named on the patent as the inventor must have, in fact, invented the invention claimed in the patent and not derived it from another.[44] For example, in the situation of Example 4 at the beginning of the handbook, Ms. B's employer is barred from filing a patent in the employer's own name, even though there had been no public use, printed publi-

---

[44] *See, e.g., New England Braiding Co., Inc. v. A.W. Chesterton Co.*, 970 F.2d 878 (Fed. Cir. 1992); *MCV, Inc. v. King-Seeley Thermos Co.*, 870 F.2d 1568 (Fed. Cir. 1989); *Transworld Mfg. Corp. v. Al Nyman & Sons, Inc.*, 750 F.2d 1552 (Fed. Cir 1984).

cation, or offer for sale more than one year prior to the date of his application. Ms. B's employer did not invent the system architecture, and, therefore, is not entitled to a patent. This is not to say, however, that Ms. B's employer cannot own or have rights in the patent (through an express or implied contract).

> **Naming of Improper Inventor Can Invalidate a Patent**
> - Application must be in name of actual inventor
> - Cannot derive invention from another

In patent law, joint inventors are considered to be a single entity, separate and distinct from the individual inventors.[45] For example, if Inventor A invents a new semiconductor device, and thereafter, Inventors A and B invent an improvement on the original semiconductor device, the work by Inventor A is generally considered to be by a different entity than the work by Inventors A and B together. However, if an invention is adequately disclosed in an earlier application, a subsequent application on the invention filed while the earlier application is still pending by any one or more of the named inventors of the first application is treated as if filed on the date of the earlier application[46] (see description of divisional, continuation, and continuation-in-part applications in the section "The Patent Application"). Further, the work of a co-worker (technology owned by the same entity that owns the invention at issue), that has not otherwise passed into the public domain (§102(a)(b)(d)(e)), cannot render the invention unpatentable for being obvious[47] (see section entitled "Obviousness").

The application for a patent must be in the name of the actual inventor (even though a company may be the owner of the patent application). Care must be taken to apply for the patent in the name of the correct inventors. There are presently provisions for correcting certain errors in the named inventorship of a patent.[48] However, it must be shown that any errors in naming the inventors arose "without deceptive intent." Thus if, for example, the president of a company, who had nothing to do with an invention, is named as an inventor or co-inventor, the patent may be invalid for failure to name the correct inventorship.

---

[45] *See Kimberly Clark Corp. v. Proctor & Gamble Distributing Co., Inc.*, 973 F.2d 911 (Fed. Cir. 1992); *In re Kaplan*, 789 F.2d 1574 (Fed. Cir. 1986).
[46] 35 U.S.C. §120.
[47] 35 U.S.C. §103.
[48] 35 U.S.C. §§116, 256; 37 C.F.R. §1.48.

First to Make the Invention

To obtain a patent, the applicant must also have been the first to have "made" the invention in the United States. The statute states:

> §102 A person shall be entitled to a patent unless—
>
> . . . .
>
> (g) before the applicant's invention thereof, the invention was made in this country by another who had not abandoned, suppressed, or concealed it. In determining priority of invention, there shall be considered not only the respective dates of conception and reduction to practice of the invention, but also the reasonable diligence of one who was first to conceive and last to reduce to practice, from a time prior to conception by the other.

The situation sometimes arises where two different inventors develop the same invention independently. In such a case, the U.S. patent law provides that the first to have "made" the invention in the United States, who did not abandon, suppress, or conceal the invention, is the person entitled to the patent. Conversely, the prior making of an invention by another, assuming that it was not abandoned, suppressed, or concealed (e.g., maintained as trade secret), can preclude obtaining a patent.[49] Where two inventors both file applications relating to the same invention, the relative priority of the inventors is determined by what is called an "interference" proceeding conducted by the PTO. It is possible that the first to file a patent application will not be the one who ultimately obtains the patent. (There are, however, certain procedural advantages which accrue to the first to file a patent application.)

The concept of the first to have "made" the invention is significant. "Making" an invention is considered to be a two-step process. The first step is *conceiving* the invention. This is basically the mental portion of the inventive act. Conception requires possession of every feature of the invention as claimed.[50] However, as will be discussed, the date of conception must be proven by more than just the inventor's word.[51] The second step is referred to as *"reducing the invention to practice."* In

> **Statutory Bar:
> First Made by Another**
>
> - Applicant must be first to have "made" and not abandoned, suppressed, or concealed the invention in the United States.
> - "Making" an invention:
>   – Conception
>   – Reduction to practice
>   – Diligence

---

[49] *See, e.g., New Idea Farm Equip. Corp. v. Sperry Corp.*, 916 F.2d 1561 (Fed. Cir. 1990).
[50] *See, e.g., Hybritech, Inc. v. Monoclonal Antibodies, Inc.*, 802 F.2d 1367 (Fed. Cir. 1986); *Coleman v. Dines*, 754 F.2d 353 (Fed. Cir. 1985); *Morgan v. Hirsch*, 728 F.2d 1449 (Fed. Cir. 1984).
[51] *See, e.g., Coleman v. Dines*, 754 F.2d 353.

basic terms, "reducing to practice" is building the invention and proving that it works for its intended purpose.[52] The filing of a patent application is considered to be a "constructive" reduction to practice.[53] The diligence of the inventor between conception and reduction to practice of the invention is also a factor as to who will win the interference. As a general proposition, if Inventor A was both the first to conceive and the first to reduce the invention to practice, Inventor A will win the interference. Further, if Inventor A was the first to conceive the invention, but the last to reduce the invention to practice, he will still win the interference if he can prove that he was "diligent" in pursuing the reduction to practice from a time period prior to the conception of the invention by Inventor B. However, if Inventor A cannot prove that he was reasonably *diligent* in pursuing the reduction to practice before Inventor B conceived the invention, Inventor B will win the interference, and will be awarded the patent.

The law of interferences is exceedingly complex, and far beyond the scope of this handbook. However, the reader should be aware of the concept of the two-step process of making an invention, and should also be aware of one all-important fact — *each aspect of the two-step process must be proven by more than just the word of the inventor*. As a basic proposition, the word of the inventor (or even co-inventors) as to when an invention was conceived or reduced to practice is worthless without "corroboration."[54] Corroboration can be in the form of dated documents, drawings, time records and oral testimony by "non-inventors."

Interference Proceeding

- First to have "made" and not abandoned, suppressed or concealed invention in U.S.
- Each element of "making" must be proven— CORROBORATION

Many independent inventors, upon conceiving an invention, will write out a written description of the invention, put the description in a sealed envelope and mail the envelope to themselves. The sealed envelope is argued to be proof of the date of conception, the postmark (showing the date of mailing) supposedly corroborating the inventor's word. This practice, without more, is *not* generally recommended. If the seal on the envelope is broken, the proof becomes suspect. Also, envelopes can often be opened and resealed without great difficulty. Thus, absent some additional proof, this method of proving a conception date is subject to attack.

The best way to ensure positive proof of a conception date is for the inventor, when an invention is conceived, to prepare a document that fully describes the invention, sign and date the description, and also explain the invention to another

---

[52] *See DSL Dynamic Sciences Ltd. v. Union Switch & Singal, Inc.*, 928 F.2d 1122 (Fed. Cir. 1991); *UMC Electronics Co. v. United States*, 816 F.2d 647 (Fed. Cir. 1987); *Newkirk v. Lulejian*, 825 F.2d 1581 (Fed. Cir. 1987).
[53] *See, e.g., Hazeltine Corp. v. United States*, 820 F.2d 1190 (Fed. Cir. 1987).
[54] *Holmwood v. Balasubramanyan Sugavanam*, 948 F.2d 1236 (Fed. Cir. 1991); *New Idea Farm Equip. Corp. v. Sperry Corp.*, 916 F.2d 1561 (Fed. Cir. 1990); *Hahn v. Wong*, 892 F.2d 1028 (Fed. Cir. 1989).

person (who cannot be considered a co-inventor) and have the person read, sign and date the description. It may also be helpful to have the document notarized.

Many companies utilize formal "invention disclosure" forms which elicit a description of the invention from the inventor, and specifically provide for dated signatures by non-inventor witnesses who have "read and understood" the disclosure. A sample invention disclosure form is provided in Appendix IV. As a practical matter, however, formal disclosure documents are generally not contemporaneous with the actual conception of an invention. Conceptions are typically first reflected in the notes and working papers of the inventor. For this reason, the importance of well-kept laboratory notebooks cannot be stressed enough. All engineers and programmers should maintain a *bound* engineering notebook. All computations, flow charts, circuit diagrams, test results, etc., should be *contemporaneously* entered into the notebook. Every entry should be signed and dated and, if possible, signed and dated by a "witness." Where software development is involved, a hard-copy listing of each iteration (at least each significant iteration) should be maintained. It is especially important that all loose papers, such as blueprints, flow charts, etc., be signed and dated. The value of an entry in a laboratory notebook as proof of conception and/or reduction to practice of an invention is directly proportional to the care which was taken to date and sign each entry and have each entry read, signed, and dated by a witness.

The context of the entry in an engineering notebook can also sometimes be used to prove a date. For example, if an entry showing conception is found in a *bound* engineering notebook, between entries dated the 3rd of January and the 5th of January, it is relevant proof that the invention was conceived sometime between the 3rd and 5th of January. It would not be so relevant, however, if a loose-leaf engineering notebook had been used.

Records should be maintained in contemplation of proving not only the dates of conception and reduction to practice, but also diligence in between. To this end, it is desirable that careful time records be kept. In addition, the documentary evidence and, in particular, dated notebook entries should describe all testing performed, the particular types of equipment used, and the results of the testing (both good *and bad*). Physical results of tests, such as samples, models, strip charts, oscillographs, or the like, should be carefully dated and retained, preferably mounted (taped or stapled) in the body of the appropriate notebook entry. All persons involved in the work should be identified in the corresponding notebook entries. In all, a documentary record should be maintained capable of establishing each of the elements of "making" an invention, as well as identifying non-inventor witnesses who can provide testimonial proof. Had Ms. B, in Example 4 at the beginning of this handbook, obtained a witness to sign and date her sketch of the system architecture, she might have won the interference and obtained her patent.

Other areas where the two-step concept of invention is of particular consequence are those of research contracts, particularly those with the federal government, and licensing agreements relating to "all improvements made during the term of the agreement."

Obviousness

In addition, the statute[55] requires that the invention *as a whole* be "unobvious" to a person of "ordinary skill in the art." To assess the non-obviousness of an invention, a number of factors must be reviewed: (1) the scope and content of prior patents and publications; (2) the "level of ordinary skill in the art" (typical education level in the pertinent area of technology); (3) the differences between the invention as claimed and the prior art; and (4) whether the invention

> **An invention is probably non-obvious if:**
> - It includes one or more new elements
> OR
> - The prior art does not suggest combining the elements of the invention

provides unexpected results, fulfills a long-felt need, and/or is commercially significant. In making this review, technology which is owned by the same entity that owns the invention at issue, and has not passed into the public domain (by virtue of §102(a), (b), (d), (e)), should not be considered. The non-obviousness of the differences is then measured, not against what was subjectively obvious to the inventor, but rather against the general knowledge of practitioners in the pertinent area of technology at the time of the invention.[56] The invention must be considered in total context and without hindsight.[57] For example, the solution to a problem may be patentable even though the solution, with the benefit of hindsight, is very simple; the identification of the problem can constitute a patentable invention.[58] As a practical matter, if one or more elements of an invention as claimed are not disclosed in prior patents or publications, or if the invention as claimed combines known elements, but no prior patent or publication expressly or impliedly suggests combining those specific elements, the invention is probably non-obvious.[59]

---

[55] 35 U.S.C. §103.
[56] *See, e.g., Ryko Manufacturing Co. v. Hu-Star, Inc.*, 950 F.2d 714 (Fed. Cir. 1991); *Custom Accessories, Inc. v. Jeffrey-Allen Industries, Inc.*, 807 F.2d 955 (Fed. Cir. 1986); *Vandenberg v. Dairy Equip. Co., Div. of DEC Int'l, Inc.*, 740 F.2d 1560, 224 U.S.P.Q. 195 (Fed. Cir. 1984); *Orthopedic Equip. Co. v. United States*, 702 F.2d 1005, 217 U.S.P.Q. 193 (Fed. Cir. 1983); *Stratoflex, Inc. v. Aeroquip Corp.*, 713 F.2d 1530, 218 U.S.P.Q. 871 (Fed. Cir. 1983); *Chore-Time Equip., Inc. v. Cumberland Corp.*, 713 F.2d 774, 218 U.S.P.Q. 673 (Fed. Cir. 1983).
[57] *Hiedlberger Druckmoschinen AG v. Hantscho Commercial Products Inc.*, 30 U.S.P.Q.2d 1377 (Fed. Cir. 1994); *In re Fritch*, 972 F.2d 1200 (Fed. Cir. 1992); *Uniroyal Inc. v. Rudkin-Wiley Corp.*, 837 F.2d 1044 (Fed. Cir. 1988).
[58] *Eibel Process Co. v. Minnesota & Ontario Paper Co.*, 261 U.S. 45, 43 S. Ct. 322 (1923); *In re Wright*, 848 F.2d 1216 (Fed. Cir. 1988).
[59] *See, e.g., In re Jones*, 958 F.2d 347 (Fed. Cir. 1992); *In re Vaeck*, 947 F.2d 488 (Fed. Cir. 1991); *Northern Telecom, Inc. v. Datapoint Corp.*, 908 F.2d 931 (Fed. Cir. 1990); *In re Laskowski*, 871 F.2d 115 (Fed. Cir. 1989); *Diversitech Corp. v. Century Steps, Inc.*, 850 F.2d 675 (Fed. Cir. 1988); *Smith Kline Diagnostics, Inc. v. Helena Laboratories Corp.*, 859 F.2d 878 (Fed. Cir. 1988); *Vandenberg*, 740 F.2d 1560; *ACS Hosp. Sys., Inc. v. Montefiore Hosp.*, 732 F.2d 1572, 221 U.S.P.Q. 929 (Fed. Cir. 1984); *In re Piasecki*, 745 F.2d 1468, 223 U.S.P.Q. 785 (Fed. Cir. 1984); *Lear Siegler, Inc. v. Aeroquip Corp.*, 733 F.2d 881, 221 U.S.P.Q. 1025 (Fed. Cir. 1984); *In re Sernaker*, 702 F.2d 989, 217 U.S.P.Q. 1 (Fed. Cir. 1983).

The Procedure for Obtaining Patent Protection

Confidentiality

The possibility of obtaining patent protection on inventions made during the course of research and development should be kept in mind from the inception of a project. *Initially, all research and development should be carefully maintained as a trade secret.* Proper records of the conception and development of the invention should be kept in order to establish the dates of conception and reduction to practice and to establish diligence, if necessary. Confidentiality agreements should be obtained from all relevant parties. If feasible, the invention should not be demonstrated or used in public, described in any printed publication, or offered for sale, until patent protection has been considered, and if to be pursued, a patent application filed.

State-of-the-Art Search

It is often advisable, when first starting out on developing a product in a given area, to have in mind the patents already held by others in that area of technology. This is done by requesting that a "state-of-the-art search" be conducted in the specific area of technology. This entails reviewing the PTO files and/or commercial databases to collect either a sampling of exemplary patents or all of the patents relating to a given area of technology. A more extensive literature search can also be done.

There is a very real benefit in being aware of the research already performed in that area. For example, the company's R & D budget will not be exhausted "reinventing the wheel." Also, the state-of-the-art search tends to identify others in the field and the active patents held by them.

It should be noted that the issued patents in the PTO files are typically on the order of two to three years behind the actual state-of-the-art. This is because of the time involved in preparing a patent application and prosecuting the application through the PTO. However, it is often the older patents which are the most valuable in showing whether or not a particular approach to solving a problem has been tried before. It should also be noted that the most pertinent documentation of software development has historically not been found in patents, but rather in other literature.

Assessing Patentability

After the product has been developed to at least a modicum of certainty, it should be reviewed for any possible patentable aspects. Each of the novel aspects of the product should be looked at singly and in combination to ascertain their patentability. In this regard, the company should obtain the opinion of a competent patent attorney.

As a general proposition, anything that is thought to be novel, that is, different from previous models, and/or competing products, should be called to the attention of the patent attorney. The inventor should not dismiss any difference as obvious without the opinion of the attorney. It must be remembered that many things which seem obvious to the inventor — because he or she is totally immersed in the subject — are not at all obvious in the patent law sense. For example, as previously mentioned, just identifying a problem and finding a solution, irrespective of how simple the solution may seem after the problem has been identified, may be patentable. The simple addition of a resistor and capacitor across the input terminals of a device can amount to a truly patentable invention if it solves an "unobvious" problem.

Suggested Procedure with Respect to Research and Development

- Do initial state-of-the-art search
- Initially maintain R & D as a trade secret
- Keep proper records to establish conception, reduction to practice, and diligence
- Consider patent protection before any public use, publication, or offer for sale
- Perform patentability search
- Perform infringement search prior to product introduction

Disclosure Materials

In general, the inventor should provide the patent attorney with the latest drawings and written descriptions of the product to work from in evaluating the patentability of the product and preparing the patent application. The invention disclosure form provided in Appendix IV may be helpful in collecting and organizing the information for the attorney.

The disclosure materials should clearly describe the problems that are solved by the device. Each feature of the product which the inventor considers to be new and different from the prior art should be identified and described. Each aspect of the product which provides an improvement over the prior models and/or the competition's products should be set forth. (This is not to say that an invention necessarily has to be better than the prior art to be patentable — it need only be different and non-obvious.) With respect to software inventions, an attempt should be made to relate the program to the physical computer system. For example, details regarding the organization of data in memory (*e.g.*, a memory map) and all variables (*e.g.*, specific registers or locations in memory corresponding to specific variables) are often helpful both in assessing the patentability of aspects of the product, identifying items to be protected, and in the actual preparation of the patent application document. Likewise, "decision logic" flowcharts at a level of detail sufficient to permit an "average" programmer to generate operative code are similarly helpful.

In addition, the inventor should also provide the attorney with copies of any literature that is in any way relevant to the issue of patentability. It is particularly important that *all* earlier versions or models of the apparatus or software be called to the attention of the attorney. Such earlier versions or models may, or may not, be prior art that must be considered. Also, any disclosure of the device to others or possible "offers for sale" should be called to the attorney's attention.

After the attorney has studied the products and prior art to identify possible patentable aspects, a patentability opinion is rendered. If a search of the PTO files has not already been made, it would be conducted prior to rendering the patentability opinion.

Occasionally, it is impossible to determine what position the PTO will take with respect to the patentability of a particular invention. In those instances, market considerations typically govern whether filing an application is warranted. Even if a patent is not ultimately granted, filing an application covering a product provides a very practical benefit. A company is permitted to mark a product with a "patent pending" notice from the time an application covering some aspect of the product is filed, until the application is abandoned or issues as a patent. (After an application issues as a patent, a patent number notice should be used.) The "patent pending" notice has no legal effect (as long as it is properly used), but does tend to inhibit potential copiers.

It should be noted that the patent law precludes intentionally using a "patent pending" or patent marking notice on any article, knowing that an application for a patent covering the article is, in fact, not pending (up to $500 fine for each offense).[60]

Infringement Search

As previously noted, because of the "exclusive" nature of the patent grant, the issue of obtaining patent protection for a product is entirely separate and distinct from the issue of whether a product infringes patents held by others. Accordingly, before making any major expenditure toward development of a new product, an infringement search is prudent to ensure that the product does not infringe any active U.S. patents held by others. Where the infringement search shows the possibility of a patent problem, the new product can sometimes be altered to avoid the problem before a major commitment is made by the company. In any event, the company is in a much better posture to negotiate the terms of a license under a patent if it has not already committed large sums of money to the particular product.

---

[60] 35 U.S.C. §292.

Preparing the Application

If the infringement search reveals no problem, a patent application is then prepared and filed with the PTO. The cost of preparing a patent application is a function of the complexity of the invention and the completeness of the disclosure material. If the attorney is given nothing more than, for example, a detailed schematic diagram of a circuit or a printout of a program, he must take the time to analyze the circuit or program and determine exactly how it operates, before he can prepare the application. Little things count. For example, it takes time for a patent attorney to look up the various part numbers of chips in a schematic. At the very least, each of the various chips on a schematic should be provided with a functional label and blocks drawn in dotted lines around the various components that cooperate to perform a particular function in the circuit. In that way, the attorney is provided with both a detailed schematic and a functional block diagram of the circuit. If a written description of the circuit operation can be provided as well, so much the better. The same consideration applies to mechanical component and software-type inventions. For example, it takes time for the attorney to generate flow charts and "memory maps" (often necessary for preparing an application) from a printout. Moreover, it is often impossible for the attorney to determine from the printout which aspects of the program are considered the invention. The particular problems that are solved and advantages of the device should also be detailed in the materials given to the attorney for his consideration.

The Patent Application

As previously noted, a patent is divided into two major sections: the written description, which teaches the public how to use the invention, and the claims, which define the particular intellectual property to which the inventor obtains rights. A patent application is, in effect, a proposed patent which is submitted to the PTO for its approval. The written description and claims submitted in the application (either in the original or in an amended form) are ultimately printed as the patent grant.

The statute requires that the application include a written description of the invention, a drawing (where necessary for understanding of the invention), and an oath or declaration by the applicant.[61]

While it is not mandatory, a particular format is recommended for a U.S. patent application.[62] Each section of the suggested format will be discussed in order.

1. Title of the Invention

The title should describe the invention in as short and specific terms as possible.

---

[61] 35 U.S.C. §§111, 112, 113, 115; 37 C.F.R. §1.51.
[62] *See* 37 C.F.R. §1.77; *Manual of Patent Examining Procedure* §608.01(a).

2. Cross References to Related Applications; Divisional, Continuation and Continuation-in-Part Applications

This section is merely a listing of prior U.S. applications, if any, which are related to the present application.

For example, a patent application will often include separate claims covering different aspects of an invention. Occasionally, the PTO will take the position that the aspects of the invention are so different that they, in fact, constitute separate inventions. It will then issue a "restriction requirement," requiring the applicant to restrict the application to one of the inventions. With respect to the "non-elected" aspects, the applicant has the option to file a "divisional" application at any time while the original (parent) application is still pending. The divisional application typically includes a written description identical to that of the "parent" application, but includes claims covering the "non-elected" aspect of the invention. The parent application would be noted as such in the "cross references" section.

A "continuation" application is an application, filed while a "parent" application is still pending, that is identical (except perhaps as to the claims) to a "parent" application. Continuation applications are often filed when an impasse is reached with the Patent Examiner. They are also filed to present new arguments regarding patentability which, for procedural reasons, cannot be considered in the parent application.

Once a formal application has been filed with the PTO, no new matter can be added to the application. In this context, "new matter" refers to new embodiments or details not described or shown in the originally filed application. In the event that further details or embodiments of the invention which, in and of themselves, warrant protection are developed after an application has been filed, a "continuation-in-part" (CIP) application may be filed. The CIP application includes an additional description of the further details or embodiments of the invention and claims relating to those new features. The claims relating to the material described in the original or "parent" application are given the benefit of the original filing date. The claims covering the additional details are given the filing date of the CIP application. A CIP application can be filed at any time before the original application issues as a patent or is abandoned.

3. Background of the Invention

This section includes a brief description of the field of art to which the invention pertains, followed by a description of the problem(s) solved by the invention, and any known prior art. Where no prior art is known at the time of preparing the application, a statement of the problem(s) solved by the invention or advantages of the invention is sufficient.

4. Summary of the Invention

This section provides a brief description of the essential elements of the invention as claimed.

5. Brief Description of the Drawing

Most patent applications include a drawing showing each element of the invention claimed. The particular format, standards, and conventions to be used in the drawing are specified in the statute and regulations.[63] This section of the application provides a brief description of each of the figures in the drawing.

6. Detailed Description of the Preferred Embodiment

This section is the primary vehicle for teaching the public how to use the invention. Each element of a "preferred exemplary embodiment" of the invention is described, with specific reference to the drawing. Each element shown in the drawing is designated in the drawing by a numeral. The designation used in the drawing is used to specify the element when mentioned in the specification.

The patent law requires that the description be in sufficient detail to permit a person "skilled in the art" to make and use the invention. Expertise in determining just how much detail is necessary in the specification is something that is acquired only by experience. As a basic proposition, however, it is desirable to include as much detail as possible in the description and to be exceedingly careful to fully describe each and every feature which is to be protected. Where an element or procedure is commercially available (or well known), it can be described as "functional black box." For example, one element of an invention could be referred to in the specification as "a filter circuit." However, the "give and take" nature of the patent must be recalled: any detail that is not disclosed in the application normally cannot be explicitly protected. For example, if an element is described in the application only as a "microprocessor," and it later becomes apparent that the only feature that actually distinguishes the invention from the prior art is the use of a particular

> The Written Description must describe the "Best Mode" of the invention in sufficient detail to "enable" the average person working in the relevant field of technology to make and use the invention.

---

[63] 35 U.S.C. §113; 37 C.F.R. §§1.81-1.88; *see also Manual of Patent Examining Procedure* §608.2.

type of microprocessor, *e.g.*, a microprocessor capable of calculating an arithmetic result and sensing the sign of the result in a single 100 nanosecond operational state (cycle), the applicant would not be able to claim that distinction, and would be forced to file a continuation-in-part (CIP) application in order to add the detailed description of the microprocessor. In the meantime, rights could be lost. This is not to say, however, if broader protection can be obtained, that the *claims* should all be limited to protecting the details of the apparatus, as will be discussed later.

Another requirement of the patent law is that the example of the invention described be of the "best mode contemplated by the inventor of carrying out his invention." Again, this reflects the "give and take" nature of the patent. The inventor must teach the public how to use the best mode of the invention contemplated by him at the time the application is prepared and filed. In other words, the inventor cannot "hold back" what he considers to be the best mode of the invention, and teach the public only how to use an inferior mode of his invention. For example, if, at the time that the application is filed, the inventor has developed a production model of a product embodying his invention, he should not describe an inferior prototype as the exemplary embodiment in the specification. The applicant is not, however, normally required to "update" the application once it is filed.

If desired, a number of alternative embodiments of the invention can be described in the patent. However, the inventor does not have to disclose all of the different variations of his invention in the specification. He is only required to disclose what is contemplated as the "best mode" at the time of filing. An alternative embodiment is generally disclosed when there is some particular feature of the alternative embodiment that in and of itself warrants protection or to help establish the range of equivalents to be accorded the claims.

7. The Claims

The claims define the rights which the inventor obtains in return for teaching the public how to use his invention. A claim is analogous to a deed to a piece of real property — it defines the boundaries of the invention, a piece of "intellectual property." However, unlike a piece of realty, boundaries of an invention cannot be measured with a transit and tape measure. The scope of an invention is not something that can be calculated and set down in precise figures. The art of drafting patent claims is one that is developed only by years of experience.

The claims of the patent define the scope of protection provided by the patent. The broader and less specific the terms of the claim, the broader the protection afforded by the patent. For another's device or process to infringe, *i.e.*, violate the patent, the device must include elements corresponding to each and every element of the patent claim. It is, therefore, desirable that the claim be written in the most general terms possible while still defining the invention. However, if the claim is written in terms which are too general, i.e., the claim is too broad, and also reads on the prior art, it is invalid. The language of the patent claims must, therefore, be drafted with the utmost precision to obtain the broadest definition of the invention without attempting to claim rights to something already in the public domain.

It is permissible to have a number of different claims in the patent application. As a matter of practice, claims of varying scope, ranging from the most general to the most specific, are submitted. In this way, if it appears after the fact that some relevant piece of prior art exists which invalidates the broad claims, the other, more specific claims are not necessarily invalidated. In this manner, the inventor not only can obtain protection on the broad aspects of his invention, but also on the specifics of the particular product that is put on the market.

8. Abstract of the Disclosure

The application also includes an abstract of the disclosure, which merely provides a summary of the description of specific preferred exemplary embodiment (as opposed to a summary of the claims).

9. The Declaration and Power of Attorney

A declaration and power of attorney form is attached at the end of the application. If feasible, this declaration and power of attorney should be signed and dated by the inventor(s) before the application is filed with the PTO. Briefly, the declaration sets forth the address and citizenship of each applicant, and whether the applicant is the sole inventor or a joint inventor of the invention as claimed. The declaration also states that the applicant(s) has reviewed and understands the contents of the application, and believes the named inventor or inventors to be the original and first inventor or inventors of the invention claimed (i.e., the actual inventors). The declaration also acknowledges a duty of the applicant(s) to disclose to the PTO all information which is material to the examination of the application (*e.g.*, all known prior art and potential statutory bars). In addition, the declaration may list the various circumstances which bar the issuance of the patent, and states that none of these circumstances have occurred.[64]

The declaration should be attached to the original copy of the application when it is signed by the inventor and, in general, that particular original application — with the declaration attached — should be filed with the PTO. However, as will be discussed, procedures have been instituted for filing the application without a declaration and then supplementing the application at a later date with the declaration (and a surcharge).[65]

---

[64] 37 C.F.R. §1.63.
[65] 37 C.F.R. §1.53.

The law is very strict with respect to the declaration. Care must be taken that no changes to the application are made after the declaration has been signed by the inventor.

10. Information Disclosure Statement

The patent applicant typically complies with the duty to provide all relevant information of which he is aware to the PTO through an "information disclosure statement," filed either with, or filed within three months of, the application.[66] It is very important that the Examiner be apprised of all relevant facts and prior art. If the most pertinent art is before the Examiner, the patent is accorded a strong presumption of validity when it is enforced. It is, therefore, desirable that the Examiner consider as much of the art as possible. On the other hand, if information is "withheld" from the Examiner, the applicant may have committed a "fraud" on the PTO. Not only would any patent obtained be invalid, but if an attempt was made to enforce the patent, the patentee could be assessed for attorneys' fees, and be subject to a counterclaim of violating anti-trust laws. When in doubt as to the materiality of the information, the safest course of action is to cite the information to the PTO.

11. Filing the Application with the Patent and Trademark Office

After the application is prepared, it is filed with the PTO. Application papers are deemed "filed" with the PTO when they are actually received by the PTO, or when they are deposited as "Express Mail" with the U.S. Postal Service, together with an appropriate certificate of mailing by "Express Mail."[67]

The filing date accorded the application by the PTO is critical with respect to determining the relevant dates of potential statutory bars and prior art. The filing date may also be the effective date of invention (*i.e.*, a constructive reduction to practice) if the invention was not actually reduced to practice prior to filing the application.[68]

Normally, if the situation permits, a complete application, including written description, claims, drawings, declaration, and filing fee, is filed to ensure obtaining the filing date. However, as previously mentioned, the application will be accorded a filing date, even in the absence of a signed declaration and the filing fee, upon filing a written description, at least one claim, and any required drawing in the name of the actual inventor or inventors[69] so long as the filing is supplemented with an executed declaration, the filing fee, and payment of a surcharge.[70]

---

[66] *See* 37 C.F.R. §§1.97., 1.98.
[67] 37 C.F.R. §1.10.
[68] *Hazeltine Corp. v. United States*, 820 F.2d 1190 (Fed. Cir. 1987).
[69] 37 C.F.R. §1.53.
[70] 37 C.F.R. §1.53(d).

When the incomplete application is received by the PTO, a Notice to File Missing Parts form is mailed to the applicant and specifies a time period in which the missing parts of the application must be filed and the requirement that the surcharge be paid.[71]

Prosecution Before the Patent and Trademark Office

After the application is received by the PTO and accorded a filing date, the application is assigned to a Patent Examiner having expertise in the particular technological area of the invention. The Patent Examiner then conducts an investigation, and searches the PTO files to determine if there is any relevant prior art in addition to that supplied by the applicant. The Patent Examiner then issues what is known as an "Office Action." In brief, the Office Action lists all of the references considered by the Examiner and indicates whether he considers the claims to be of proper form, and whether he considers the claims to be anticipated by the prior art or rendered obvious by the prior art. The PTO mails the Office Action to the attorney, and the attorney immediately forwards it, with copies of the references cited, to the inventor.

A response to the Office Action (assuming one is necessary) should be filed within three months of the mailing date of the Office Action. The inventor typically provides the attorney with an analysis of the references, and the attorney then drafts the response. The response must answer each and every issue raised by the Examiner by traversing (arguing against) the Examiner's positions, amending the claims, or canceling the claims (that is, accepting the Examiner's rejection). In effect, the attorney negotiates with the Patent Examiner to determine the exact scope of the claims to which the inventor is entitled.

Generally, when the Office Action is received by the inventor, the inventor should analyze the Office Action and references and report back to the patent attorney to facilitate preparation of the response. Any errors in the positions taken by the Examiner in the Office Action, *e.g.*, mischaracterization of the references, should be identified. For each claim, and each rejection, the differences between the subject matter described in each individual reference and (1) the "claim language" and (2) the preferred embodiment described in the specification should be identified. If the Examiner has rejected the claims as obvious over a combination of references, the inventor should also identify any reasons why the references cannot be combined as suggested by the Examiner, and establish or confirm that the references do not suggest that it would be desirable to make the modification or combination of features suggested by the Examiner. In addition, the inventor should then assume for the purposes of argument that it is permissible to combine or modify the references as suggested by the Examiner and identify the differences between modified or combination references as suggested by the Examiner and (1) the claim language and (2) the preferred embodiment described in the specification.

---

[71] The amount of the surcharge is set forth in 37 C.F.R. §1.16(e).

If a response cannot be filed within the initial three-month period, it is possible to file a response to an Office Action at any time up to six months from the date of the Office Action. However, a cumulative fee must be paid to the PTO for each month after the initial three-month period.[72]

It must be stressed that it is the language of the *claims* that is controlling in arguing against a rejection; differences between the references cited and the preferred exemplary embodiment described in the specification are not controlling. The response must explain to the Examiner how the specific language of the claims is distinguished from the references. The *claims*, however, can be amended to include any detail described in the specification.

After the Examiner agrees with respect to the exact scope of the claims, the application issues as a patent.

Design Patent Protection

The patent statute also provides for obtaining a so-called "design patent" for protecting the ornamental appearance of a product. Design patent protection also has been held applicable to information icons for the display screen of a program computer system, so long as the icon is an integral part of the operation of a program computer (rather than merely a displayed picture).[73]

In general, the same considerations as noted above with respect to utility patents apply to design patents. To be patentable, a design must be new, original, and ornamental.[74] In the context of the statute, "original" means that the design must originate with the patentee (as opposed to being derived from another). "Ornamental" requires that the particular features of the design to be protected not be functional.[75] In addition, a design is not patentable if the differences between the subject matter of the design and prior designs are such that the design *as a whole* would be obvious at the time the design was made to a "designer of ordinary skill."

Design Patent
- Protects ornamental appearance of product
- New, original, and ornamental — not functional
- Design as a whole not obvious
- Term 14 years

---

[72] 37 C.F.R. §1.136.
[73] *See Ex parte Strijland*, 26 U.S.P.Q.2d 1259 (PTO Board of Appeals and Interferences, 1992).
[74] 35 U.S.C. §171.
[75] *See Lee v. Dayton-Hudson Corp.*, 838 F.2d 1186 (Fed. Cir. 1988).

The term of the design patent is 14 years. A design patent typically includes a drawing showing views of each side of the product having an ornamental feature, followed by a single, formalized claim.

In testing whether the single, formal claim of a valid design patent is infringed, the issue is typically whether the ordinary prospective purchaser or user of the product, "giving it the amount of attention that such a purchaser or user would be expected to give," would be likely to mistakenly assume that the article in question was of the patented design.[76] The test assumes that the ordinary person is aware of the patented design and does *not* call for a side-by-side comparison. Basically, the test is on the overall appearance of the accused design.

In addition to the usual remedies for infringement of a patent, the statute provides that the design patentee can recover the total profit made by the infringer on the infringing product, in lieu of actual damages.[77]

Enforcing a Patent

The patent statutes provide that anyone who "makes, uses or sells" any patented invention in the United States, actively induces infringement of a patent, or knowingly contributes to an infringement, is liable for damages to compensate for the infringement (no less than a reasonable royalty), plus interest and costs.[78] Contributory infringement occurs where a party sells a component of a patented machine or process knowing that that component is specially made or is specially adapted for use in the infringement of the patent, and the article in question is not a staple of commerce suitable for substantial non-infringing use.[79] Inducement of infringement occurs where one intentionally aids or suggests (*e.g.*, by giving instructions for use of a device) the direct infringement of a patent by another.[80] Activities in the United States that would otherwise be inducing or contributory infringement, constitute infringement even if the ultimate "infringement" occurs outside of the United States.[81]

---

[76] *Gorham v. White*, 81 U.S. 511, 528 (1971); *Braun, Inc. v. Dynamics Corporation of America*, 975 F.2d 815 (Fed. Cir. 1992); *Oakley, Inc. v. International Tropic-Cal, Inc.*, 923 F.2d 167 (Fed. Cir. 1991); *Avia Group International, Inc. v. L.A. Gear California, Inc.*, 853 F.2d 1557 (Fed. Cir. 1988); *FMC Corp. v. Hennesey Industries, Inc.*, 836 F.2d 521 (Fed. Cir. 1987); *Litton Systems, Inc. v. Whirlpool Corp.*, 728 F.2d 1423 (Fed. Cir. 1984).

[77] 35 U.S.C. §289.

[78] 35 U.S.C. §§271, 284.

[79] *See CR Bard, Inc. v. Advanced Cardiovascular System, Inc.*, 911 F.2d 670 (Fed. Cir. 1990); *Hewlett Packard Co. v. Bausch & Lomb, Inc.*, 909 F.2d 1464 (Fed. Cir. 1990); *Lumnis Industries, Inc. v. DM&E Corp.*, 862 F.2d 267 (Fed. Cir. 1988); *Hodosh v. Block Drug Co.*, 833 F.2d 1575 (Fed. Cir. 1987); *Dana Corp. v. American Precision Co.*, 827 F.2d 755 (Fed. Cir. 1987).

[80] *See, e.g., Hewlett Packard v. Bausch & Lomb*, 909 F.2d 1464 (Fed. Cir. 1990); *Water Technologies Corp. v. Calco Ltd.*, 850 F.2d 660 (Fed. Cir. 1988); *Orthokinetics, Inc. v. Safety Travel Chairs, Inc.*, 806 F.2d 1565 (Fed. Cir. 1986); *Powerlift, Inc. v. Lang Pools, Inc.*, 774 F.2d 478 (Fed. Cir. 1985).

[81] 35 U.S.C. §271(f).

A patent is enforced by bringing suit in an appropriate U.S. district court.[82] As a general proposition, suit can be brought in the district court for any jurisdiction where the accused infringer resides, or has committed acts of infringement and has a regular and established place of business. For a corporate defendant, the corporation is deemed to "reside" in any judicial district in which it is subject to personal jurisdiction.[83]

In the past, an appeal from the decision of a district court was taken to one of the eleven U.S. circuit courts of appeals. A difficulty which often arose in litigation was that the judges involved typically had no technical background and often had no contact with the patent system. In addition, each of the different appeals circuits had its own body of law interpreting the patent statutes. The interpretation of the law in some of the circuits was more favorable to the patentee than in others. Accordingly, great care was taken to choose the best possible court in which to bring the suit. Since October of 1982, however, appeals in patent cases no longer go to the individual circuit courts of appeals, but rather are now heard by the U.S. Court of Appeals for the Federal Circuit (CAFC). As a result of this change in the law, enforcement of patents has become more uniform across the nation, and the particular forum in which the case is heard has taken on less significance. In addition, the judges in the CAFC are, in general, familiar with the patent laws, and either have technical backgrounds themselves, or have technical advisers available to them.

Remedies for Patent Infringement

The patentee is entitled to damages for the infringement[84] and possibly an injunction against the infringer[85] and, in exceptional cases, reasonable attorneys' fees.[86]

Damages for patent infringement are intended to compensate the patentee for the infringement, and must be, at a minimum, at least equal to a reasonable royalty.[87] To the extent it can be proven, compensatory damages include any income that the patentee would have made, "but for" the infringement. Compensatory damages can include lost profits, "convoyed sales," and the results of price erosion.[88]

> Damages are intended to compensate the patent owner for income that would have been made, but for the infringement.

---

[82] 28 U.S.C. §1338.
[83] 28 U.S.C. §§1391(c), 1400, 1694; *In re the Regents of the Univ. of Cal.*, 964 F.2d 1128, 1132 (Fed. Cir. 1992); *V.E. Holding Corp. v. Johnson Gas Appliance Co.*, 917 F.2d 1574, 1584, 16 U.S.P.Q.2d 1614 (Fed. Cir. 1990), *cert. denied*, 111 S. Ct. 1315 (1991).
[84] 35 U.S.C. §284.
[85] 35 U.S.C. §283.
[86] 35 U.S.C. §285.
[87] 35 U.S.C. §284.
[88] *Beatrice Foods Co. v. New England Printing & Lithographing Co.*, 899 F.2d 1171 (Fed. Cir. 1990); *Smithkline Diagnostics Inc. v. Helena Laboratories Corp.*, 926 F.2d 1161 (Fed. Cir. 1991); *Minnesota Mining & Manufacturing Co. v. Johnson & Johnson Orthopaedics, Inc.*, 976 F.2d 1559 (Fed. Cir. 1992).

To obtain lost profits, the patentee must prove: (1) there is a demand for the patented product, (2) there are no acceptable non-infringing alternatives, (3) it has capacity to satisfy the additional demand created if the defendant is forced to leave the market, and (4) the amount of profit it would have made from the sales lost to the infringer.[89]

As a general proposition, damages can be obtained only with respect to infringement of the patent, occurring during the term of the patent. Damages are typically not awarded for sales prior to the grant of a patent or after expiration of a patent. However, compensatory damages can cover "convoyed sales," sales of products or services not actually covered by the patent, but that were lost because of the defendant's infringement. A typical example is after market parts sales and service or maintenance contracts.

As noted above, the minimum damages are a reasonable royalty, that is, the royalty a willing licensor and a willing licensee would have agreed to at the time infringement began. Factors to be considered include the profitability of the product, established royalties in the industry, and the length of time the patent has to run.[90]

In addition, the court can, at its discretion, increase damages by up to a factor of three.[91] Increased damages, however, are typically awarded only when there has been willful infringement or some form of misconduct.[92]

However, damages for any infringement committed more than six years prior to instituting the suit cannot be recovered.[93] Nor can damages be recovered from an infringer who did not have either actual or constructive notice of the patent. Constructive notice is provided by placing the word "patent" and then the patent number on each article sold by the patentee that is covered by the patent. If such a patent marking is not on the devices, an infringer is not liable for damages unless he has actual notice of the patent,

> Patent Marking provides constructive notice of the patent.

that is, it can be proven that he actually knew that the patent existed.[94] The patent marking requirement relates back to the basic proposition that any hardware that is not patented can be freely used and copied by others (absent some contractual obligation, or a likelihood of confusion as to the source or origin of the goods).

---

[89] *Smithkline Diagnostics Inc. v. Helena Laboratories Corp.*, 926 F.2d 1161 (Fed. Cir. 1991); *Minnesota Mining & Manufacturing Co. v. Johnson & Johnson Orthopaedics, Inc.*, 976 F.2d 1559 (Fed. Cir. 1992).
[90] *Radio Stell & Mfg. Co. v. MTD Products, Inc.*, 788 F.2d 1554 (Fed. Cir. 1986).
[91] 35 U.S.C. §284.
[92] *Read Corp. v. Portec, Inc.*, 970 F.2d 816 (Fed. Cir. 1992); *Braun Inc.. v. Dynamics Corporation of America*, 975 F.2d 815 (Fed. Cir. 1992); *Minnesota Mining & Manufacturing Co. v. Johnson & Johnson Orthopaedics, Inc.*, 976 F.2d 1559 (Fed. Cir. 1992).
[93] 35 U.S.C. §286.
[94] 35 U.S.C. §287; *see also, e.g., Devices for Medicine, Inc. v. Boehl*, 822 F.2d 1062 (Fed. Cir. 1987).

An innocent party might copy a product if he found the product on the market apparently not covered by a patent. For this reason, a patent marking is effective only if it is put on essentially every apparatus sold.

Provisions also are made for a patent holder to bring an action before the International Trade Commission (under Section 337 of the Tariff Act of 1930, as amended by the Trade Acts of 1974 and 1979) to prevent importation of articles infringing the patent. The ITC has the power to bar the importation of goods into the United States which "unfairly compete" with "an efficiently and economically operated" domestic industry, where injury or a tendency for injury occurs. One form of "unfairly competing" is the infringement of a valid U.S. patent, or the importation of articles made by a process covered by a U.S. patent.[95]

Post Issuance Actions

Under the present law, maintenance fees must be paid at various intervals throughout the term of the utility patent to keep the patent in force. The basic term of the utility patent is 17 years from the date that the patent issues. At $3^1/_2$, $7^1/_2$, and $11^1/_2$ years after the patent issues, maintenance fees must be paid to the PTO. The fees must be paid either before the date due, or, upon payment of a late charge, within 6 months thereafter. If the maintenance fee is not paid, the patent expires. There are, however, provisions in the statute which permit revival of a patent which has lapsed due to nonpayment of the maintenance fees under certain circumstances.[96] No maintenance fee is required for a design patent.[97]

Reexamination

Unlike the law of many countries, the U.S. patent laws do not provide for any proceeding directly analogous to trademark opposition or cancellation proceedings (through which a party can actively participate in opposing the grant of a patent). However, a limited "reexamination" proceeding can be initiated in the PTO with respect to an issued U.S. patent by any party (including the patent owner).[98]

A reexamination process is initiated by filing a request for reexamination, together with a fee set by regulation (a portion of which is refunded if the request for reexamination is denied, as will be explained). The request for reexamination must include a statement showing that a "substantial new question of patentability" exists with respect to at least one claim. A "substantial" new question of patentability exists where prior art patents or publications are shown to be material to at least one claim and the same questions of patentability have not been

---

[95] 19 U.S.C. §1337(a).
[96] 35 U.S.C. §41(c).
[97] 35 U.S.C. §41(b).
[98] 35 U.S.C. §§301-307; 37 C.F.R. §1.525-1.565.

decided by the PTO during a previous examination of the claim. The "new questions of patentability" must be based upon prior patents or printed publications. Issues of prior use or prior sale cannot be raised.

The PTO then considers the reexamination request and, within three months, determines whether or not a substantial new question of patentability has been raised by the request. This initial determination is based solely upon the reexamination requested and no submission by the patent owner is permitted. If the PTO determines that a new question of patent-ability is raised by the request, an order for reexamination of the patent is issued. If no substantially new question of patentability is found, the reexamination proceeding is terminated and the requester is refunded a portion of the initial fee.

After a reexamination order issues, the patent owner is permitted to file a statement in response to the reexamination request and to propose amendments to the claims. The patent owner is not permitted to enlarge the scope of the claims of the patent over the original claims or introduce any new matter during the reexamination proceedings. If the patent owner files a statement, the requester is then permitted to file a reply.

The PTO then proceeds with an expedited *ex parte* examination of the patent claims with respect to prior art patents and publications. These proceedings are strictly between the PTO and the patent owner. While the requester is entitled to receive copies of all papers filed during the further proceedings, no submissions by the requester are permitted.

Upon conclusion of the *ex parte* examination, the PTO issues a reexamination certificate, which, among other things, cancels any claims determined to be unpatentable, confirms any claims determined to be patentable, and incorporates into the patent any amended or new claims found to be patentable. The reexamination certificate is mailed to both the patent owner and to the requesting party.

Advantages of Obtaining a Patent

The patent grant provides a number of substantial benefits. As a general proposition, any product which is *not* covered by the claim of a patent is fair game for the competition, so long as there are no contractual obligations or likelihood of confusion as to the source or origin of the respective product. The only mechanism for protecting against an independent development of an invention is by obtaining a patent. In this sense, a patent is necessary to adequately protect an investment in research and development. Also, a patent on an improvement to a basic invention can sometimes be used to offset patents held by others on the basic invention through cross-licensing (*e.g.*, the chair *versus* the stool).

A patent is demonstrative evidence of expertise in the technological area of the invention. This can often be a great aid in obtaining contracts with, for example, the federal government. Moreover, a patent can also be the source of a substantial royalty income, through institution of a licensing program.

A patent is also a demonstrative asset which aids in obtaining capital from investors and obtaining loans from commercial institutions.

Practical Considerations with Respect to Software Inventions

While a patent is often the most desirable form of protection for software, certain practical matters must be considered. Meaningful patent protection for a purely software product tends to be relatively expensive and is sometimes difficult to obtain. It is sometimes difficult to define the inventive concept of a software product and, when necessary, to describe a program in terms of a hardware system without gravely limiting the scope of the patent claims. Also, the "new and unobvious" requisites for patentability are, of course, applicable to programs.

Another limiting factor on the applicability of patent protection to software products tends to be the time factor involved in obtaining a patent. It may take several years from the time a patent application is filed until a patent actually issues. There are procedures available in certain circumstances for accelerating the examination of a patent application by the PTO. However, even accelerated examination of an application in most areas of technology typically entails a period of between one and two years. During the period the patent application is pending, a "patent pending" notice provided on the product tends to inhibit potential copies. *However, no enforceable rights are provided until the patent is actually granted.* A practical problem arises in that the market life of many software products is itself less than several years. The time required to obtain an enforceable patent can thus exceed the product life of the product, making the patent protection ultimately afforded of questionable value.

For this reason, in practice, patent protection tends to be viable for a purely software product only where: (1) the product is sufficiently valuable to warrant the expense; (2) it embodies a *definable* inventive concept; (3) the market life of the concept is sufficiently long or the concept tends to recur in many programs or generations of programs; (4) the concept either does not involve a mathematical algorithm or can effectively be defined in terms of hardware; and (5) the concept meets the requisites for patentability.

Product life notwithstanding, other benefits accruing to obtaining a patent may be an overriding consideration. Also, since a patent is the only effective protection against development of a concept by others, in some circumstances it may be desirable to patent a software product as a defensive measure against others.

Copyright Protection

The copyright law of the United States has undergone a number of recent changes. Major revisions in the copyright law were enacted in the Copyright Act of 1976 (Title 17 U.S.C.), which became effective on January 1, 1978. Under the 1976 Copyright Act, a copyright arises automatically as soon as an "original work of authorship" becomes "fixed" in a tangible form of expression. In other words, copyright protection is secured automatically as soon as the "work" is "fixed" in a form which can be read or visually perceived either directly or with the aid of a machine or device. Copyrightable "works of authorship" include booklets, advertising brochures, artistic designs, maps and architectural blueprints, "phono-records," including audio tapes and records, and, at least to some extent, computer programs. However, copyright protection is expressly not available for ideas, methods, systems, mathematical principles, formulas, and equations.

Securing a Copyright

- Arises automatically as soon as work is "fixed" in tangible form
- Upon publication:
  - Copyright notice desirable but no longer necessary
  - Deposit
- Registration not a prerequisite for protection, but is for enforcement

---

[99] *See* 17 U.S.C. §101.

Neither publication nor registration is necessary to secure copyright protection under the 1976 Act. In addition, as of March 1, 1989, the United States became a signatory to the Berne Convention for the Protection of Literary and Artistic work. In compliance with the Berne Convention, most of the formalities involved in securing and maintaining a copyright, including that of the copyright notice, as will be discussed below, have been relaxed.

Ownership of a Copyright

Typically, the author (creator, originator) of a work owns the copyright.[99] However, if the work qualifies as a "work for hire," then the employer of the creator, or the entity that commissioned the work, is considered to be the author and holder of the copyright.[100] *To be a work for hire the work must either: (1) have been prepared by an employee within the scope of the employee's duties; or (2) fall within one of certain specified categories of works, be especially ordered or commissioned, and be the subject of an express written agreement specifying that it will be a work for hire.*[101] The specified categories include: collective works (a work including a number of contributions each constituting a separate and independent work which is assembled into a collective whole); audio visual works, such as motion pictures and phono records; compilation works (a work formed by the collection and assembly of pre-existing materials or of data that are selected, coordinated, or arranged in such a way that the resulting work as a whole constitutes an original work); supplementary works (works prepared as a secondary adjunct to another work, *e.g.*, illustrations, forewords or afterwards); instructional text, tests, and test answers; translations; and atlases. The requirements to qualify as a work for hire are very strictly construed. Unless the creator qualifies as an employee, and the work is created within the scope of employment, the existence of an express written agreement specifying that the work is a work for hire is imperative.[102] Employee status is determined under the law of agency and is based upon such factors as: the skill required to do the work; where the work is done (*e.g.*, at the facility of the entity that commissioned the work?); who supplies the facilities and tools; the right to assign additional work; discretion over when and how long to work; who hires and pays the creator's assistants; whether the creator is a separate business entity; the provision of employee benefits; and tax treatment (are social security and income tax withheld?).[103] While no single factor is determinative, as a practical matter, unless the creator is treated as an employee for tax and social security purposes, the person

---

[100] 17 U.S.C. §§101, 201(b).
[101] U.S.C. §101.
[102] *See, e.g., Community for Creative Nonviolence v. Reid,* 490 U.S. 730 (1989).
[103] *See Community for Creative Nonviolence v. Reid,* 490 U.S. at 751-752; *MacLean Assoc., Inc. v. Mercer-Meidinger Hanson, Inc.,* 21 U.S.P.Q.2d 1345 (3d Cir. 1991).

is likely to be deemed an independent contractor and the owner of the copyright in the absence of a written agreement.

As discussed below, even if a work does not qualify as a work for hire, a party commissioning a work can still obtain ownership of the copyright by assignment. There is, however, a practical difference between obtaining the copyright by assignment and being the author by virtue of work for hire; assignments by individual authors are subject to a right of termination.[104]

It should also be noted that, with respect to a periodical or other "collective work," the copyright to the compilation of works is separate and distinct from the copyright in each separate contribution. The copyright in the separate contribution is thus initially with the originator of the contribution (unless it is a work for hire, in which case the person commissioning the work is considered the author).

Absent agreement to the contrary, authors of a joint work (a work prepared by two or more authors with the intention that the respective contributions be merged into inseparable or interdependent parts of a unitary work) are co-owners of the copyright. Each co-author owns a proportionate share of the copyright and, in the absence of an agreement, is entitled to contribution, *i.e.*, a share of any royalties received from licensing. A joint owner may generally use or license the use of the work without the consent of co-owners, but must account to them for their shares of profits derived from any license to a third party. Potentially, contribution to other co-owners may be required for use of the copyrighted work by a particular co-owner.[105]

The author of a work can assign a copyright to another. However, the assignment requires a written agreement[106] which must be recorded in the copyright office in order to be effective against a subsequent recorded transfer to a party that did not have notice of the earlier transfer and that paid a valuable consideration for the copyright.[107]

However, under the statute,[108] any license or transfer of right in a copyright in other than a work made for hire, may be subject to a right of termination that cannot be assigned; during a 5 year period beginning 35 years after the transfer, the author, or the author's heir, may terminate the rights granted. Termination, however, does not require the grantee to cease use of derivative works that were prepared under the authority of the grant before it was terminated,[109] but preparation of further derivative works is not permitted.

---

[104] 17 U.S.C. §203.
[105] *See Weissman v. Freeman*, 684 F. Supp. 1248, 1259-60 (S.D. N.Y. 1988); *Crosney v. Edward Small Productions, Inc.*, 52 F. Supp. 559 (S.D.N.Y. 1942); *Jerry Vogel Music Co., Inc. v. Miller Music Inc.*, 74 N.Y.S.2d 425 (N.Y. App. Div. 1947), aff'd, 299 N.Y. 782, 82 U.S.P.Q. 458 (1949).
[106] 17 U.S.C. §204.
[107] 17 U.S.C. §205(d).
[108] 17 U.S.C. § 203.
[109] 17 U.S.C. §203(b)(1).

Scope of Protection

The owner of a copyright on a "work" has the exclusive right to reproduce the copyrighted work; to prepare derivative works based upon the copyrighted work; to distribute copies of the copyrighted work to the public by sale, rental, lease, or lending; and to publicly display or perform the copyrighted work (in the case of musical, dramatic, etc., type works).

> **A Copyright Gives the Exclusive Right to:**
> - Reproduce the work
> - Prepare derivative works
> - Distribute copies to the public
> - Publicly display or perform

These rights, however, afford only very limited protection. The statute expressly states that a copyright protects only the expression of ideas, not the ideas themselves.[110] A classic example of the nature of copyright protection is found in the case of *Baker v. Selden*.[111] Mr. Baker, an accountant, wrote a book describing a double entry accounting system that he had developed. Mr. Selden, also an accountant, bought the book and began using the double entry accounting system developed by Mr. Baker. Mr. Baker contended that the use of his accounting system by Mr. Selden constituted copyright infringement. The Supreme Court, however, disagreed. The use of the ideas described in a copyrighted work does not constitute infringement of the copyright. It is for this reason, in Example 1 at the beginning of this handbook, that Ackman's copyright was ineffective to stop other companies' use of his 3-D display programming techniques in their products.

> **Copyright protects only expression of an idea – not an idea itself.**

The expression versus idea dichotomy gives rise to particularly interesting questions when attempts are made to apply copyright protection to non-textual aspects of a work. Which aspects of an audio-visual work, *e.g.*, a television commercial, are copyrightable expression—and which are uncopyrightable ideas? Non-textual aspects of audio-visual works that have been found to be copyrightable artistic expression include a combination of such things as: background; a particular montage style of rapid close-ups of a particular model; a model's attire and hairstyle; camera angles; and framing. As will be discussed, a similar conundrum occurs with respect to determining which aspects of a computer program other than literal code constitute protectable expression as opposed to non-copyrightable idea.

---

[110] 17 U.S.C. §102(b).
[111] *Baker v. Selden*, 101 U.S. 99 (1979).

> To establish an infringement, a copyright owner must prove copying of protectable expression.

In addition, a copyright only protects against copying of a work; it gives no protection whatsoever against another independently developing the work. To establish a copyright infringement, a plaintiff must prove ownership of a valid copyright and "copying" of protectable expression by the defendant.[112]

Copying is typically inferred from proof of access to the copyrighted work and substantial similarity as to protectable expression between the accused and copyrighted works.[113] Thus, even if programs are identical in every respect, there is no copyright infringement if there was no copying, *i.e.*, the subsequent program was independently developed.

For this reason, it is very important that appropriate records of developmental efforts be generated and maintained. For evidentiary purposes, it is recommended that a hard copy of each version of a program throughout its development be generated, signed, and dated by a witness (preferably someone not directly involved in the development). The records should be retained for at least three years after the product is placed on the market, and preferably retained for the lifetime of the product plus three years.[114]

The copyright is also subject to a number of limitations set out in the statute,[115] including the doctrine of fair use, compulsory licensing in certain instances, and a number of limitations pertaining to computer programs including so-called archival rights.[116]

The Fair Use Limitation

The limitation of most general applicability is the "fair use" limitation, which permits copying "for purposes such as criticism, comment, news reporting, teaching (including multiple copies for classroom use), scholarship, or research . . . ."[117]

There is no litmus test to determine whether a particular use of a copyrighted work is a permitted fair use or a copyright infringement. However, the statute specifies a number of factors to be considered. These factors include: the purpose and character of the use (*e.g.*, whether the use is of a commercial nature or for nonprofit educational purposes); the nature of the copyrighted work; the amount and substance of the

---

[112] *Feist Publications v. Rual Telephone Service Co.*, 111 U.S. 1282 (1991); *Atari Games Corp. v. Nintendo of America*, 975 F.2d 832, 837 (Fed. Cir. 1992); *Brown Bag Software v. Symantec Corp.*, 960 F.2d 1465, 1472 (9th Cir. 1992); *SOS, Inc. v. Payday, Inc.*, 886 F.2d 1081, 1085 (9th Cir. 1989).

[113] *Atari, Inc. v. North Am. Philips Consumer Elec. Corp.*, 672 F.2d 607 (7th Cir. 1982), *cert. denied*, 103 S. Ct. 176 (1982).

[114] The statute of limitations with respect to copyright actions is three years from the date the claim accrued (typically interpreted to be when the copyright holder should have become aware of the purported infringement). *See* 17 U.S.C. §507(b).

[115] 17 U.S.C. §§107-112.

[116] 17 U.S.C. §117.

[117] 17 U.S.C. §107.

> **"Fair Use" Can be Made of Copyrighted Works**
>
> **Factors to be considered:**
> - Commercial or nonprofit use
> - Nature of copyrighted work
> - Portion of work copied
> - Effect of use on market for or value of work

portion used in relation to the copyrighted work as a whole; and the effect of the use upon the potential market for or value of the copyrighted work.[118] As a rule of thumb, if neither the value of the work nor the market for the work is affected by a use of the work, it is a fair use.

Limitations on the Scope of Copyright Protection of Software

As previously noted, copyright protection is available for "works of authorship," including booklets, advertising brochures, artistic designs, maps and architectural blueprints, phonorecords[119] and, at least to a limited extent, computer programs. However, ideas, methods, systems, mathematical principles, formulas, and equations are not copyrightable.

Historically, there was much debate as to whether software was a "work of authorship," and thus qualified for copyright protection. It is well settled that copyright protection is applicable to human-readable software, such as flow charts, documents, machine-readable *source code* representations of a program, and

> **Works of Authorship:**
> - Literary
> - Musical
> - Dramatic
> - Pantomimist/choreographic
> - Pictorial, graphic & sculptural
> - Motion pictures & other audio visual
> - Sound recordings

audiovisual displays in game programs. In a number of cases in the federal courts, it has been argued that a video game as a whole is an audiovisual work, and is protectable as an "expression" of the game.[120] Similarly, copyright infringement has been found based upon copying of the audiovisual screens (*e.g.*, menus) of a program.[121] Other courts have, however, expressly rejected the proposition that the

---

[118] *See, e.g., Harper & Rowe, Publishers v. Nation Enter.*, 471 U.S. 539 (1985); *20th Century Music v. Aiken*, 422 U.S. 151 (1975); *Sega Enterprises, Ltd. v. Accolade, Inc.*, 977 F.2d 1510 (9th Cir. 1993); *Atari Games Corp. v. Nintendo of America, Inc.*, 975 F.2d 832 (Fed. Cir. 1992); *New Kids on the Block v. News AM. Publishing*, 971 F.2d 302 (9th Cir. 1992); *Lewis Galoob Toys, Inc. v. Nintendo of America, Inc.*, 22 U.S.P.Q.2d 1857 (9th Cir. 1992); *Narell v. Freeman*, 872 F.2d 907 (9th Cir. 1989); *Fisher v. Dees*, 794 F.2d 432 (9th Cir. 1986); *American Geophysical Union v. Texaco, Inc.*, 24 U.S.P.Q.2d 1796 (S.D. N.Y. 1992).

[119] "Phonorecords," including audio tapes and records, are covered by special provisions of the copyright law, but will not be dealt with in this handbook.

[120] *Midway Mfg. Co. v. Dirkschneider*, 543 F. Supp. 466, 214 U.S.P.Q. 417 (D. Neb. 1981); *Atari, Inc. v. Amusement World, Inc.*, 547 F. Supp. 222, 215 U.S.P.Q. 929 (D. Md. 1981); *Stern Elec., Inc. v. Kaufman*, 523 F. Supp. 635, 213 U.S.P.Q. 75 (E.D. N.Y. 1981), aff'd, 669 F.2d 852, 213 U.S.P.Q. 443 (2d Cir. 1982).

[121] *Manufactures Technologies, Inc. v. Cams, Inc.*, 706 F. Supp. 984, 10 U.S.P.Q. 1321 (D. Conn. 1989); *Broderbund Software, Inc. v. Unison World, Inc.*, 648 F. Supp. 1127, 231 U.S.P.Q. 700 (N.D. Cal. 1986).

screens, *per se*, are covered by a copyright on the underlying program code; copyright infringement by copying the screens would require the screens to be the subject of a separate copyright registration.[122]

Historically, the courts have drawn a distinction between *object code* and source code representations of a computer program. Questions have been raised as to whether object code representations of a program (not intended for communication to humans, but rather for direct communication to machines), are even within the scope of the copyright statutes; at least one federal court has taken the position that object code programs are not copyrightable.[123] Others, however, have adopted the contrary position that object code programs are copyrightable.[124] Historically, the courts were also divided as to whether a copyright on a source code program is sufficient to protect an object code version of the program,[125] and as to the copyrightability of firmware and microcode.[126] "Firmware" is defined for the purposes of this discussion as software in hardware form; *i.e.*, program information stored in a physical medium such as Read Only Memory (ROM). "Microcode" is defined as encoded instructions controlling the details of execution of one or more primitive functions of the computer.

In more recent cases, however, the courts have found (or assumed) object code and microcode programs copyrightable, irrespective of storage in a physical device such as a ROM.[127]

Practical Considerations with Respect to Software Works

The most important limitation on the scope of copyright protection, as it applies to software, however, is the nature of the copyright itself. As previously discussed, the basic maxim of the copyright law is that the copyright law protects works of authorship but:

> "in no case does copyright protection for an original work of authorship extend to any idea, procedure, process, system, method of operation, concept, principle, or discovery, regardless

---

[122] *Digital Communications Assoc. v. Softklone Distrib. Corp.*, 659 F. Supp. 499, 2 U.S.P.Q. 1385 (N.D. Ga. 1987).
[123] *Data Cash Sys., Inc. v. JS&A Group, Inc.*, 480 F. Supp. 1063, 203 U.S.P.Q. 735 (N.D. Ill. 1979); *aff'd on other grounds*, 628 F.2d 1038, 208 U.S.P.Q. 197 (7th Cir. 1980).
[124] *Apple Computer, Inc. v. Formula Int'l, Inc.*, 725 F.2d 521, 221 U.S.P.Q. 762 (9th Cir. 1984); *Apple Computer, Inc. v. Franklin Computer Corp.*, 714 F.2d 1240, 219 U.S.P.Q. 113 (3d Cir. 1983); *Williams Elec., Inc. v. Artic Int'l, Inc.*, 685 F.2d 870, 215 U.S.P.Q. 405 (3d Cir. 1982); *GCA Corp. v. Chance*, 217 U.S.P.Q. 718 (N.D. Cal. 1982); *Midway Mfg. Co. v. Artic Int'l, Inc.* 547 F. Supp. 999 (N.D. Ill. 1982); *Tandy Corp. v. Personal Micro Computers, Inc.*, 524 F. Supp. 171, 214 U.S.P.Q. 178 (N.D. Cal. 1981).
[125] *GCA v. Chance*, 217 U.S.P.Q. 718; *Data Cash*, 480 F. Supp. 1063; *Apple v. Franklin*, 714 F.2d 1240.
[126] *Apple v. Franklin*, 714 F.2d 1240; *Williams*, 685 F.2d 870; *NEC Corp. v. Intel Corp.*, 645 F. Supp. 590, 1 U.S.P.Q.2d 1492 (N.D. Cal. 1986); *GCA v. Chance*, 217 U.S.P.Q. 718; *Tandy*, 524 F. Supp. 171; *Data Cash*, 480 F. Supp. 1063.
[127] *See, e.g., Sega Enterprises, Ltd. v. Accolade, Inc.*, 977 F.2d 1510 (9th Cir. 1993); *Atari Games Corp. v. Nintendo of America, Inc.*, 975 F.2d 832 (Fed. Cir. 1992); *Computer Associates, Int'l, Inc. v. Altai, Inc.*, 23 U.S.P.Q.2d 1241 (2d Cir. 1992); *Johnson Controls v. Phoenix Control Sys., Inc.*, 886 F.2d 1173 (9th Cir. 1989).

of the form in which it is described, explained, illustrated, or embodied in such work."[128]

Thus, a copyright protects only the author's particular form of expression and does *not* extend to the underlying idea or concept of the program. The copyright, in essence, protects the owner against *actual* copying of substantial portions of the program code by others.

A copyright does not in any way protect the owner from independent creation of a similar program by another, even if the other is generally aware of the copyrighted program. A competitor can, in general, study a copyrighted program,

---

Copyright Protection of Software

- No protection against independent development
- No protection against copying functionality
- Has been held to protect against direct translation from one language to another
- Structure-Sequence-Organization; Screens: protective if categorized as expression as opposed to idea, or dictated by function

---

determine the central concept and basic methodology of the program, then write its own program to accomplish the same results. In practice this is often done using so-called "clean rooms." It was for this reason, in the hypothetical, that Ackman was unsuccessful in enforcing his copyright against conceptually similar competing games.

Further, the extent to which a copyright protects against the copying of non-literal aspects of a program such as the modularity, organization structure, or sequence of instructions tends to vary as a function of the particular court addressing the issue. At one extreme, it is clear that (absent patent protection or contractual obligation) the functionality of a copyrighted program can be freely copied.[129]

On the other hand, some courts have found that a *direct* translation from a high to a lower order language (or *vice versa*) or from one high order language to another is a derivative work.[130]

---

[128] 17 U.S.C. §102(b).
[129] *Eckes v. Card Prices Update*, 736 F.2d 859, 222 U.S.P.Q. 762 (2d Cir. 1984); *Atari, Inc. v. North Am. Philips Consumer Elec. Corp.*, 672 F.2d 607, 214 U.S.P.Q. 33 (7th Cir. 1982); *Atari, Inc. v. Williams*, 217 U.S.P.Q. 746 (E.D. Cal. 1981).
[130] *GCA Corp. v. Chance*, 217 U.S.P.Q. 718 (N.D. Cal. 1982); *Synercom Technology, Inc. v. University Computing Co.*, 462 F. Supp. 1003, 1013, 199 U.S.P.Q. 537 (N.D. Tex. 1978).

The issue of whether a particular non-literal aspect or feature of software is protected by a copyright on the software is a function of whether the particular aspect or feature is categorized as "expression" and thus copyrightable, or as an "idea" or "dictated by function" and thus uncopyrightable.[131] The breadth of copyright protection as applied to non-literal aspects of software varies from court to court. There have been a number of cases which have tended to accord relatively broad protection to non-literal aspects of software.[132] Other cases, while recognizing that some non-literal elements of a program may be copyrightable, have taken a much more restricted view of those non-literal elements of software that are subject to copyright protection. These cases have for the most part considered each level of abstraction (ranging from the individual instructions to a hierarchy of modules to the functionality of modules, to the overall functionality) individually, and denied protection to any aspect of a program dictated by function or considerations of efficiency, required by factors external to the program itself, or taken from the public domain.[133]

In addition, it is now generally accepted that the audio/visual aspects of program screens (user interfaces) are copyrightable as audio/visual works.[134] However, it is not universally accepted that a copyright registration of the underlying program code that generates the displays extends to the screen displays generated by the program; arguably, the screens must be subject to a separate copyright. It is prudent to consider copyright protection of the various screens separately from the copyright protection of the underlying program code; it may be advantageous to register copyrights on the respective screens as audio/visual works separate and apart from the program code.[135]

---

[131] *Johnson Controls, Inc. v. Phoenix Control Sys., Inc.*, 886 F.2d 1173, 1175 (9th Cir. 1989); *Plains Cotton Coop. Ass'n v. Goodpasture Computer Serv.*, 807 F.2d 1256, 1269 (5th Cir. 1987); *Lotus Dev. Corp. v. Paperback Software Int'l*, 740 F. Supp. 37 (D. Mass. 1990); *Synercom*, 462 F. Supp. 1003.

[132] *Johnson Controls, Inc. v. Phoenix Contol Sys., Inc.*, 886 F.2d 1173 (9th Cir. 1989); *Whelan Associates, Inc. v. Jaslow Dental Laboratory, Inc.*, 797 F.2d 122 (3d Cir. 1986); Cert. denied, 479 U.S. 1031 (1987); *Broderbund Software, Inc. v. Unison World, Inc.*, 687 F. Supp. 1127 (N.D. Cal. 1986); *SAS Institute, Inc. v. S&H Computer Systems, Inc.*, 605 F. Supp. 816 (M.D. Tenn. 1985).

[133] *Computer Associates Int'l, Inc. v. Altai, Inc.*, 982 F.2d 693, 23 U.S.P.Q.2d 1241 (2d Cir. 1992); *Atari Games Corp. v. Nintendo of America, Inc.*, 975 F.2d 832 (Fed. Cir. 1992); *Brown Bag Software v. Symantec, Inc.*, 22 U.S.P.Q.2d 1429 (9th Cir. 1992); *Johnson Controls, Inc. v. Phoenix Control Sys., Inc.*, 886 F.2d 1173 (9th Cir. 1989); *Plains Cotton Coop. Ass'n v. Good Pasture Computer Service, Inc.*, 807 F.2d 1256, 1 U.S.P.Q.2d 1635 (5th Cir. 1987), *cert. denied*, 108 S. Ct. 80 (1987); *Manufacturers Technologies, Inc. v. KAMS, Inc.*, 706 F. Supp. 984 (D. Conn. 1989); *Telemarketing Resources v. Symantec Corp.*, 12 U.S.P.Q.2d 1991 (N.D. Cal. 1989); *Digital Communications Assoc. v. Softklone Distrib. Corp.*, 659 F. Supp. 499, 2 U.S.P.Q. 1385 (N.D. Ga. 1987); *Bronderbund Software Inc. v. UnisonWorld, Inc.*, 64 F. Supp. 1127 (N.D. Cal. 1986); *Q-Co Industries v. Hoffman*, 625 F. Supp. 608 (S.D. N.Y. 1985).

[134] *See, e.g., Closed Development Corp. v. Paperback Software Int'l*, 740 F. Supp. 37 (D. Mass. 1990).

[135] *Digital Communications Assoc. v. Softklone Distrib. Corp.*, 659 F. Supp. 449 (N.D. Ga. 1987).

Right to Make Archival and Transitory Copies

The scope of copyright protection accorded to computer programs is additionally limited by specific provisions in the statute.[136]

> §117. Limitations on exclusive rights: Computer programs.
>
> Notwithstanding the provisions of section 106, it is not an infringement for the owner of a copy of a computer program to make or authorize the making of another copy or adaptation of that computer program provided:
>
> (1) that such a new copy or adaptation is created as an essential step in the utilization of the computer program in conjunction with a machine and that it is used in no other manner, or
>
> (2) that such new copy or adaptation is for archival purposes only and that all archival copies are destroyed in the event that continued possession of the computer program should cease to be rightful.
>
> Any exact copies prepared in accordance with the provisions of this section may be leased, sold, or otherwise transferred, along with the copy from which such copies were prepared, only as part of the lease, sale, or other transfer of all rights in the program. Adaptations so prepared may be transferred only with the authorization of the copyright owner.

At least one court, however, has read Section 117 to pertain only to inputting a copy into a machine and to "destructible" copies.[137] (It appears that the court interpreted the statute to fit what it perceived as the equities of the case: the defendant provided disks containing programs printed in plaintiff's magazine to plaintiff's subscribers in competition with plaintiff.)

Other courts have interpreted Section 117 to preclude prohibitions against disassembly by rightful holders of copies.[138] In at least one subsequent case, however, the protection of Section 117 was limited to owners of copies of the software, as distinguished from mere licensees.[139]

It can also be argued on the basis of Section 117 of the statute, that once a copyrighted program is sold, the copyright owner cannot prevent the purchaser from adapting the program to other machines (CPUs) owned by the purchaser. A corol-

---

[136] 17 U.S.C. §117.
[137] *Micro-Sparc, Inc. v. Amtype Corp.*, 592 F. Supp. 33, 223 U.S.P.Q. 1210 (D. Mass. 1984).
[138] *Vault Corp. v. Quaid Software, Ltd.*, 847 F.2d 255 (5th Cir. 1988).
[139] *MAI Systems Corp. v. Peak Computer*, 991 F.2d 511, 26 U.S.P.Q.2d 1458 (9th Cir. 1993).

lary argument, however, also arises that the copyright owner *can* stop someone who does not rightfully "own" a copy of the program (*i.e.*, a licensee) from making such "adaptations."

Fair Use as Applied to Computer Programs

The application of the doctrine of fair use, particularly when applied in conjunction with a recognition of the utilitarian nature of software, also has tended to limit the scope of copyright protection for software. The fair use doctrine has been held to permit disassembly of a program for the purposes of reverse engineering, *i.e.*, study or examination, so long as the copy disassembled was rightfully obtained.[140]

Publication

While publication is no longer necessary to secure statutory copyright protection, publication is still an important concept. Several significant consequences follow from publication of the work: works published before March 1, 1989, must include "proper copyright notice;" a deposit of copies with the Library of Congress becomes mandatory; and various time periods begin to run.

Under the Copyright Act, a work is published upon distribution of, or an offer to distribute, copies of the work to the public by sale or other transfer of ownership, or by rental, lease, or lending. In this context, the "public" means any person who is under no explicit or implicit restrictions with respect to disclosure of the contents of the work. If a document is distributed *under a proprietary notice* to licensees or the like, it is not "published" under the Copyright Act.

Notice

Until adoption of the Berne Convention, a proper copyright notice was required on all published works. Indeed, omitting or misplacing the copyright notice was fatal to obtaining copyright protection for works prior to the effective date of the 1976 act. As to works subject to the 1976 law, however, omission of or error in the copyright notice on a publication does not necessarily invalidate the copyright — *if* an application for registration of the copyright on the work was made before the publication, or is made within five years after the publication, and a reasonable effort is made to add proper notice to all of the copies that are distributed to the public after discovery of the omission or error. Under the Berne Convention, a copyright notice is no longer necessary on works published after March 1, 1989.

---

[140] *Sega Enterprises, Ltd. v. Accolade, Inc.*, 977 F.2d 1510 (9th Cir. 1993); *Atari Games Corp. v. Nintendo of America, Inc.*, 975 F.2d 834 (Fed. Cir. 1992); *Lewis Galoob Toys, Inc. v. Nintendo of America, Inc.*, 22 U.S.P.Q.2d 1857 (9th Cir. 1992).

The Berne Convention notwithstanding, it remains advantageous that all published copies of a work bear a notice of copyright. Access to a copy of the work bearing a proper copyright notice precludes interposition of an "innocent infringement defense."[141] Basically, the notice of copyright includes three elements: the copyright symbol ©, the word "copyright," or the abbreviation "Copr."; the named owner of the copyright; and the year of first publication of the work. An example of a copyright notice can be found at the beginning of this handbook.

> **There Are Three Forms of Copyright Notice Acceptable Under the Statute—No Longer Required, But Desirable:**
>
> ©1994 Michael A. Lechter
> Copyright 1994 Michael A. Lechter
> Copr. 1994 Michael A. Lechter

There are various requirements as to where the copyright notice must be placed on the work.[142] However, in general, the placement of the notice should be sufficient if it is placed in a prominent position on the work, in a manner and location as to "give reasonable notice of the claim of copyright." Care should be taken, however, not to include a date of publication in a notice on an unpublished work, *e.g.*, software distributed under a trade secret license.

> **A standard copyright notice should not be used with unpublished works—like software marketed under trade secret licenses. Consider using a provisional notice such as:**
>
> This is an unpublished work protected under the copyright laws of the United States and other countries.
> All rights reserved. Should publication occur, then the following notice shall apply:
>
> © 1994 MICHAEL A. LECHTER

Term

The term of the copyright for all works created after January 1, 1978, is the author's life plus an additional 50 years after the author's death. The term for a work for hire is 75 years from publication or 100 years from creation, whichever is shorter.

---

[141] 17 U.S.C. §401(d) (1988).
[142] 37 C.F.R. §201.20.

Deposit

Under the new law, there is a requirement that two copies of the work be deposited in the Copyright Office for the use of the Library of Congress within three months of publication of any work bearing notice of copyright. Where a program is not copy protected, only one complete copy of the "best edition" must be filed.[143] However, while failure to make the deposit can give rise to fines and other penalties, it does not affect the copyright protection itself, and special relief from the deposit requirement can be applied for through the copyright office.[144]

Registration

Except in the case of publication with omission of a proper copyright notice on works first published before March 1, 1989, copyright registration is not a prerequisite for copyright protection. However, registration is significant in three respects. A registration is normally necessary before the copyright on works originating in the United States can be enforced, that is, before an infringement suit may be filed in court.[145] If the registration is made before publication, or within five years after publication, the mere fact of registration establishes the validity of the copyright and of the facts stated in the copyright certificate in court.[146] Also, the copyright statute provides for "statutory damages and attorneys' fees" which may range, according to the circumstances, from $500 (in the case of an innocent infringer) to up to $100,000 (in the case of the willful infringer).[147] If a registration is made within three months after publication of the work or prior to the infringement of the work, the copyright owner has the option to elect to take statutory damages instead of the actual damages and profits that he can prove, as well as attorneys' fees.[148] Unless made within three months after the publication of the work, a registration not made until after the infringement only entitles the copyright owner to be awarded the damages and profits that can actually be proven.[149]

Procedure for Obtaining a Registration

A registration is obtained by filing (in the same envelope or package) the appropriate completed application form, a specified fee for each application, and two complete copies of the work.

There are different application forms for different types of works. For example, Form TX must be used for published and unpublished nondramatic literary works, while Form VA must be used for published and unpublished works of the visual arts (pictorial, graphics, etc.). Form TX should be used with respect to

---

[143] 37 C.F.R. §202.19(d)(2)(vii).
[144] 37 C.F.R. §202.19(e).
[145] 17 U.S.C. §411.
[146] 17 U.S.C. §410.
[147] 17 U.S.C. §504.
[148] 17 U.S.C. §505.
[149] 17 U.S.C. §412.

applications pertaining to program code, while Form VA should be used with respect to the screen output (user interfaces) of programs as visual arts. The Copyright Office is very exacting with respect to the forms. Not only must the proper form be chosen, but the form must be an original form printed and issued by the Copyright Office. The Copyright Office will not accept photographic reproductions of the forms. The Copyright Office also insists that the application fee and complete deposit copies be sent together in the same envelope or package.

With respect to works first published after January 1, 1978, two complete copies of the "best" edition must be filed. If the work was first published in the United States before January 1, 1978, two complete copies of the work as first published must accompany the application. Under the Copyright Office regulations, special provisions are made for deposit of "identifying portions" of machine-readable works, in lieu of two complete copies.[150] More specifically, for unpublished works which are fixed, and published works which are published only in machine readable form, other than a CD-ROM format, the deposit may take any of the following forms:

> The first and last twenty-five pages or equivalent units of the source code, together with the page or equivalent unit containing the copyright notice. However, with respect to revised versions of computer programs, if the revisions do not occur in the first and last twenty-five pages, the deposit must consist of the page containing the copyright notice and any fifty pages of source code representative of the revised material. Trade secret material within the first and last twenty-five pages of source code can be blocked out or redacted, provided that the blocked out portions are proportionately less than the material remaining, and the deposit reveals an appreciable amount of original computer code;

> The first and last ten pages or equivalent units of source code without blocked out portions;

> The first and last twenty-five pages of object code, together with any ten or more consecutive pages of source code within no blocked out portions;

> With respect to copyright claims in a revision that is not contained in the first and last twenty-five pages of source code, the deposit shall consist of either twenty pages of source code representative of the revised material with no blocked out portions, or any fifty pages of source code representative of the revised material with portions

---

[150] 37 C.F.R. §202.20-21.

of the source code containing trade secrets blocked out, again provided that the blocked out portions are proportionately less than the remaining material, and an appreciable amount of original computer code remains.

Where work is fixed in a CD-ROM format, the deposit must consist of one complete copy of the CD-ROM, together with any accompanying operating software, an instruction manual, and a printed version of the work embodied in the CD-ROM, if the work is fixed in print.

Deposit Requirement for Machine-Readable Software:

- Identifying portions
- Keep documentation on version of program from which the identifying portions are taken

The deposit of only "identifying portions" of lengthy programs which can often be the equivalent of over a thousand pages in length has given rise to another area of controversy. Programs tend to be dynamic products; improvements are constantly being made. Thus, the question arises as to which particular version of a program the identifying portion was taken from. It is, therefore, prudent for the software developer to maintain proper documentation to protect against possible controversy.

Trademark Protection

A trademark (or service mark) is used to identify the source or origin of a product (or service)—that is, a trademark distinguishes goods or services of one company from those of another. It is through a trademark that a customer connects the goodwill and reputation of the company to its products. Under the law, a competitor is prevented from capitalizing on a company's reputation and goodwill by passing off possibly inferior goods as those made by the trademark owner. Thus, in a manner of speaking, proper use of a trademark can protect the sales value of the reputation of the company and the product, as well as investments in advertising and other promotional activities used to develop goodwill. However, trademark protection does not prevent the competition from copying or reverse engineering the trademark owner's product unless the competition misrepresents or creates confusion as to the source or origin of the products (or copies a feature of the product having "secondary meaning," as will be discussed later).

Trademark

- Identifies source of goods — protects reputation
- Protects as long as used with goods
- No protection against copying or reverse engineering, unless confusion as to source of goods

---

Acquiring Rights

In the United States, trademark rights are acquired through use of the mark in legal commercial transactions. That is, a company simply adopts a proper mark, begins to use it commercially, and through that use acquires proprietary rights in the mark. In general, the first to use a given mark in connection with particular goods in a given geographical area obtains the exclusive right to the mark for use with those goods in that area. Once the mark is used in interstate commerce (or a good faith bona fide intent to use the mark in interstate commerce is formed), a federal registration may be obtained.

> **Acquiring Trademark Rights**
> - By filing application based on intent to use
> - By use of mark with goods
> - The first to use a mark or file an "intent-to-use" application obtains the rights

Under common law, as a general proposition, the first to use a given mark in connection with particular goods or services in a given geographical area obtains the rights in the mark for use with those goods or services in the geographical area.

"Use" of a trademark requires physical association of the mark on or in connection with the product or service. With a trademark, it is sufficient to apply the mark to labels or tags affixed to the product or to the containers for the product, displays associated with the product, or the like. "Trademark" usage cannot be established through use of the mark solely in advertising or product brochures. However, if services are involved, rather than a physical product, use of a mark in advertising is a proper usage for a "service mark" (a mark used in sales, advertising, or services to identify the source of the services).

Prior to the Trademark Law Revision Act of 1988 (enacted November 16, 1988; effective November 16, 1989), obtaining a federal registration, while providing constructive notice and many procedural advantages, did not generate any substantive rights in the mark; all rights were based upon actual use of the mark. This, however, has been changed under the Trademark Law Revision Act of 1988. After November 16, 1989, substantive rights can be created by filing an application for registration based upon a bona fide intent to use the mark.[151] Once a registration based upon an intent to use is obtained, the registrant is accorded a "constructive use" priority, effectively equivalent to actual use of the mark on the date of the application for registration.

---

[151] 15 U.S.C. §1057(c).

> **"Intent To Use" Trademark Application**
> - Requires bona fide intent to use
> - Provides "constructive use"—it is as if actual use began on the date of filing
> - A verified statement of actual use must be filed within six months of notice of allowance, with specimens
>   - Time period can be extended for fee
>   - Can convert to application based on actual use at any time prior to notice

The intent-to-use provisions of the law make it important that a business be particularly careful about disclosing ideas for new marks—it is important that security be maintained to prevent others from winning a race to the PTO. It is also important that careful records be kept to show good faith intent to use the mark.

Choosing a Mark

There are certain basic guidelines with respect to choosing a mark. A symbol or word that cannot effectively identify the source of the goods cannot be used as a trademark. For example, putting a label "oscilloscope" on an oscilloscope does not identify the origin of the oscilloscope. The protection afforded by a particular trademark is a direct function of the "distinctiveness" of the mark; that is, how closely associated the mark is with the source of the product, as opposed to the product itself. Marks can be categorized with respect to the degree of protection accorded by the mark, as "generic," "descriptive," "suggestive," and "fanciful" ("coined" or arbitrary).

A "generic mark" uses a term that refers to (or has come to be understood as referring to) the genus of the particular product, *i.e.*, the mark "oscilloscope" used with an oscilloscope apparatus. A generic term does not serve to identify the source of the goods, and, therefore, cannot be utilized as a trademark.

A "descriptive mark" is a term which conveys an immediate idea of the ingredients, qualities, or characteristics of the goods. It describes the intended function, purpose, or use of the goods, size of the goods, class of user of the goods, effect upon the user, and the like. A descriptive term is just one step removed from a generic term. An example would be using the trademark "electronic" for an oscilloscope apparatus. However, a descriptive term can possibly come to be associated with a particular manufacturer and, thus, serve as identification of the origin of the goods. In trademark parlance, the initially descriptive mark has acquired a "secondary meaning." Absent such secondary meaning, a descriptive term does not accord a great deal of protection.

A "suggestive mark" requires imagination, thought and perception to conclude the nature of the goods from the term used as the mark. For example, "Waveshape" would be a suggestive term when used with an oscilloscope.

The highest degree of trademark protection is provided through the use of a "fanciful" ("coined") term or arbitrary term. A fanciful term is a word created strictly and entirely for use as a trademark. For example, the mark "IZLOT" would be a fanciful term if used as a trademark for an oscilloscope. An arbitrary term is a common word used in a "fanciful sense." For example, "Bigfoot" would be an "arbitrary" mark when used for an oscilloscope.

It should be noted, however, that a misspelled word or a term combining commonly used words is not a "fanciful" or "coined" word. Acronyms, initialisms, abbreviations, phonetic variations, and foreign words all afford the same protection as the corresponding correctly spelled English word.

It should be apparent that a given term may be generic in one market and arbitrary in another market; for example, the mark "oscilloscope" for an oscilloscope apparatus is generic. However, the mark "oscilloscope" for chewing gum is arbitrary. Terms can, however, change from one category to another. At one time "escalator," "cellophane," "aspirin," and "shredded wheat" were valid trademarks. However, through improper use, these marks became associated with the goods in general, that is, became a generic term for the goods. This is the reason that some companies are fighting a continual war against people who are improperly using their trademarks. In the past, some goods that have found themselves in a generic status have, in effect, made a comeback. For example, the marks "Goodyear" and "Singer" at one time were considered to be generic, but eventually reacquired the status of protectable trademarks.

The strongest word mark (as opposed to a symbol mark) is a relatively euphonious, easily pronounced, coined word that does not include components commonly used in marks. It is desirable that the mark be simple—a simple mark is more easily protected. Where a mark includes a large number of elements, there is the possibility that another could adopt some of, but not all of, the elements of the mark and avoid infringing the mark. If both a word mark and a symbol mark are adopt-

> **Choosing a Mark**
>
> - The mark must identify the source of goods
> - Simple design and/or coined word are best
> - A trademark search should be performed before major expenditures

ed, they should, if possible, be completely separate whenever used, to ensure that each can be protected separately. It should also be noted that a simple mark is more easily remembered by purchasers. Also, it has been found that a mark that can be depicted and put into words is more easily remembered than a mark that can only be depicted or verbalized, but not both.

It should be apparent that a company does not want to choose a mark and expend large sums in advertising and so forth, only to learn that some other company has proprietary rights in the use of that mark. If the company begins using a mark on a product that is so similar to a mark already in use by another company on similar goods and/or services that there is a "likelihood of confusion" as to the source of the product, the company has in all likelihood violated state unfair competition common laws, as well as the federal trademark law.[152] As will be discussed later, this can have rather dire consequences.

Accordingly, before a company adopts a mark for a product or service, it is prudent to undertake an investigation to ensure that no one else is using the particular mark. That is, the company should have a "trademark search" performed. Basically, this involves examining trademark registration files maintained at the PTO to see whether any similar mark is already registered to another, or an application has been made for registration of a similar mark for similar goods and/or services.

"Confusingly Similar"

Potential trademark problems arise when the proposed trademark is "confusingly similar" to another mark, *i.e.*, it so resembles the other mark that it is likely to cause confusion as to the source of the particular goods involved. Three rule-of-thumb criteria for determining whether or not a mark resembles another are:

1. Do the marks look alike?
2. Do the marks sound alike? and
3. Do the marks have the same meaning or suggest the same thing?

The similarities and dissimilarities of the goods themselves must also be considered. In this regard, the manner of marketing the goods is relevant.

Do the respective goods move in the same channels of trade? Are they sold in the same type of store? Are they bought by the same people? What degree of care is likely to be exercised by the purchasers?

---

[152] The Lanham Act, 15 U.S.C. §1051, *et seq.*

> **Likelihood of Confusion**
>
> - Look alike
> - Sound alike
> - Same meaning or connotation
>   – Nature of goods

Trademarks, when used on products purchased by relatively sophisticated purchasers, are less likely to cause confusion as to the source of goods, than when used on goods typically sold to unsophisticated purchasers. The ultimate answer as to whether marks are "confusingly similar" is the cumulative effect of the differences and similarities in the marks and in the goods or services.

Federal Registration

Common law rights in a trademark inure to the user immediately upon use of the mark in a legal, commercial transaction. Even without registration of the trademark, the owner of a mark is entitled to prevent others from using a confusingly similar mark for related goods in the geographic area in which the rights are established. However, the owner of a common law (unregistered) mark is typically not protected against a third party in a remote geographical area (*e.g.*, a distant state) who, without knowledge of the prior use of the mark by the owner, subsequently adopts the mark and acquires valid common law rights to the mark in the remote area. As will be apparent from the following discussion, there are a number of very substantial benefits to registering a mark with the PTO.

> A federal registration can be obtained for any proper mark actually used in interstate commerce, or with bona fide intent to use.

In general, under the old law, a proper mark that has been used (sold or transported) in *interstate* commerce ("commerce which may lawfully be regulated by Congress") and is not "confusingly similar" to a mark already being used by another is eligible for registration with the PTO.

After November 16, 1989, an application for registration of a mark may also be filed on the basis of a good faith, bona fide intention to use the mark in commerce.[153] To obtain a registration, however, actual use of the mark must commence within a predetermined period (six months, extendible to one year upon request, and up to 24 additional months for good cause) of a notice of allowance from the PTO indicating that subject to a proper showing of the use in commerce, the mark is entitled to registration.[154] An application based on an intent-to-use will establish constructive use of the mark as of the filing date of the application. This creates trademark rights that are superior to any other, unless the other (1) actually used the mark prior to the filing date, (2) filed an intent-to-use based application

---

[153] 15 U.S.C. §1051(b) (1988).
[154] 15 U.S.C. §1051(d) (1988).

prior to the filing date; or (3) can claim a treaty priority date based on a corresponding foreign trademark application.[155]

The PTO maintains two separate registers: the "Principal Register" and the "Supplemental Register." Registration on the Principal Register is most desirable, and provides a number of procedural and substantive advantages, as will be explained. However, registration on either register provides a number of very valuable rights.

The holder of a mark registered on either the Principal or Supplemental Register can sue in a federal district court for "Trademark Infringement" any time there is any unauthorized use in interstate commerce of a mark which so resembles the registered mark as to be likely to cause confusion or mistake, or to deceive the public as to the source of the goods.[156] Not only can an injunction against further use of the mark be obtained[157] but, subject to the principles of equity, the registrant can also recover all of the *profits* made by the infringer on the goods, any actual damages sustained due to the infringement (*e.g.*, loss of sales), and the costs of the infringement action. To recover the infringer's profits, the registrant is only required to prove the defendant's sales. The infringer then must prove all of the elements of cost. The court can, however, vary the award to an amount that it finds to be just according to the circumstances of the particular case.[158] In addition, all of the infringer's labels, packages, advertisements, and other material bearing the infringing mark must be destroyed.[159]

> **Principal Register**
> Any mark capable of distinguishing source of goods, unless:
> - Immoral, deceptive
> - Confusingly similar
> - Merely descriptive or misdescriptive of goods

The primary difference in an infringement action concerning a mark on the Supplemental Register, as compared to a suit for a mark on the Principal Register, is that the registrant must prove that he, in fact, has the exclusive right to the mark (*e.g.*, that the mark is distinctive and identifies the registrant as the source of the goods). As an aside, any person who believes that he is likely to be damaged by use of a "false" (counterfeit) mark can also sue in federal court for any damages caused by the "false" mark.[160]

---

[155] 15 U.S.C. §1126 (1988).
[156] 15 U.S.C. §1114(1).
[157] 15 U.S.C. §1116.
[158] 15 U.S.C. §1117.
[159] 15 U.S.C. §1118.
[160] 15 U.S.C. §1125(a).

Registration on either register also provides the additional, very practical benefit of tending to provide *actual* notice of the mark to would-be users. In the first place, marks on both the Principal and Supplemental Registers are available to the Trademark Examiners and can thus, as will be explained, prevent someone else from obtaining a registration on a confusingly similar mark. In addition, the mark may show up in any investigations made by a company prior to adopting a mark, causing the company to reconsider adopting the mark.

> **Supplemental Register**
> - Any mark capable of distinguishing source of goods but, *e.g.*, "merely descriptive"
> - In actual use
> - After "secondary meaning" is acquired, the name can be registered on principal register

Registration on the Principal Register also provides various additional substantive and procedural advantages. In addition to providing actual notice of the mark, registration of a mark on the Principal Register also provides constructive notice of the registrant's claim of ownership of the mark.[161] This prevents a third party in a remote geographical area from subsequently adopting and obtaining rights in the mark. Some case law, however, is to the effect that there is no "likelihood of confusion" as to the source of goods if the registrant is not doing business in the remote geographical area. Under those cases, the subsequent user will not be enjoined from using the mark until the registrant begins doing business in the same geographical area.

Registration of the mark on the Principal Register is prima facie evidence of the validity of the registration, the registrant's ownership of the mark, and the registrant's exclusive right to use the mark in commerce in connection with the goods or services specified in the certificate.[162] In addition, if an affidavit is filed with the PTO to the effect that the mark has been used continuously for five consecutive years subsequent to the date of registration and is still being used in interstate commerce,[163] the registered mark is incontestable and can be attacked only on certain limited bases.[164]

Once a mark is registered on the Principal Register, it can be filed with the U.S. Customs Service to prevent any article of imported merchandise which copies or simulates the trademark from entering the country.[165]

---

[161] 15 U.S.C. §1072.
[162] 15 U.S.C. §1057(a), (b).
[163] 15 U.S.C. §1065.
[164] 15 U.S.C. §1115(b).

Any mark capable of distinguishing the goods of one company from those of another can be registered on the Principal Register unless the mark:

(a) includes immoral, deceptive, or scandalous matter or matter which may disparage or falsely suggest a connection with persons living or dead, institutions, beliefs, or national symbols, or bring them into contempt or disrepute;

(b) includes the flag or coat of arms or other insignia of the United States, or of any State or municipality, or of any foreign nation, or any simulation thereof;

(c) includes the name, portrait, or signature of a particular living individual or a deceased president during the life of his widow, unless by consent;

(d) is "confusingly similar" to the mark of another; that is, "consists of or comprises a mark which so resembles a mark registered in the U.S. Patent and Trademark Office, or a mark or trade name previously used in the United States by another and not abandoned, as to be likely, when applied to the goods of the applicant, to cause confusion, to cause mistake, or to deceive";

(e) consists of a mark which, when applied to the goods of the applicant, is merely descriptive or deceptively misdescriptive of such goods;

(f) consists of a mark which, when applied to the goods of the applicant, is primarily geographically descriptive or deceptively misdescriptive of the goods; or

(g) consists of a mark which is primarily merely a surname.[166]

Any mark in actual use that is capable of distinguishing the applicant's goods or services, but is not registerable on the Principal Register because it is "merely descriptive" of the goods, a geographical origin of the goods, or a surname, can be registered on the Supplemental Register.[167] For purposes of registration on the Supplemental Register, a mark can consist of any trademark, symbol, label, package, configuration of goods (such as the shape of a bottle), name, word, slogan, phrase, surname, geographical name, device, or a combination thereof, so long as

---

[165] 15 U.S.C. §§1124, 1125(b); 19 C.F.R. §133.
[166] 15 U.S.C. §1052.
[167] 15 U.S.C. §1091.

the mark is capable of distinguishing the applicant's goods or services from those of others and is not utilitarian or directed by the function of the goods (*i.e.*, ornamental). In other words, the trade dress—shape of packaging, color combinations, and so forth—can be registered on the Supplemental Register. It must, however, be trademark use, to distinguish the goods, and not trade name use.

Registration on the Supplemental Register does not preclude registration on the Principal Register.[168] Indeed, if a descriptive mark becomes "distinctive" of the applicant's goods in interstate commerce and actually identifies the applicant as the originator of the goods to the public, i.e., achieves secondary meaning, the mark can be registered on the Principal Register. In this regard, substantially exclusive and continuous use of the mark in commerce for five years is considered *prima facie* proof that the mark is "distinctive."[169] It is not necessary that such marks be first registered on the Supplemental Register, or that they necessarily must be in use for five years. If it can be demonstrated that an otherwise "descriptive" mark has acquired a secondary meaning which identifies the company as the origin of the goods, the mark can be immediately registered on the Principal Register. "Distinctiveness" of the mark can be proven by testimony, surveys, and other evidence of recognition by the public.

There are also provisions for concurrently registering confusingly similar marks to different parties in different geographical locations. Concurrent registrations are generally issued only when the parties involved establish that they have become entitled to use the mark as the result of concurrent, lawful use in commerce prior to the earliest of the filing dates of the applications or when a court has determined that more than one person is entitled to use the same or similar marks in commerce.[170]

Registering a Trademark

Once a bona fide, good faith intention to use a mark in interstate commerce can be alleged, an application for registration of the mark may be filed. As noted above, if the mark is properly chosen, it can be registered on the Principal Register. To prepare a trademark application, an attorney will need the following information:

1. The name and citizenship of the applicant. If the applicant is a partnership, the citizenship of the general partners is required. If the applicant is a corporation or an association, the state or nation where it is organized must be specified.

---

[168] 15 U.S.C. §1095.
[169] 15 U.S.C. §1052.
[170] 15 U.S.C. §1052.

2. The domicile and post office addresses of the applicant.

3. The name of the person who will ultimately sign the trademark application. If the applicant is a company, the person signing the application must actually be an officer of the corporation, with signatory authority. Both name and title should be provided.

4. A description (*i.e.*, the identity) of the goods or services for which the mark is presently being used and the manner in which the mark is being (or is contemplated to be) used in connection with the goods or services (*i.e.*, affixed as a tag, on the packaging, etc.). The description of the goods and services on which the mark is in use must be entirely accurate. Inclusion of any goods or services in the application on which the mark is not currently in use at the time of an application based on actual use can result in the registration being held invalid. Likewise, particular care must be taken in describing the goods or services in an intent-to-use application; understating the goods can cause loss of rights. Additionally, discrepancies between the goods stated in the intent-to-use application and those on which the work is actually ultimately used can cause severe complications in examination or result in denial of a registration.

5. If the application is based on an intent to use:

   (a) A drawing of the mark. Care should be taken that the drawing depict the mark precisely as it ultimately will be used. Discrepancies between the mark as shown and the mark as actually used can preclude registration.

6. If the application is based on actual use:

   (a) The date of the first actual use of the mark with the goods or services in interstate commerce. Generally "use in interstate commerce" requires movement of a product bearing the trademark across state lines. There are, however, provisions for obtaining a trademark registration based upon a prior foreign registration or application for registration, without requiring use in U.S. commerce.

   (b) The date of first actual use of the mark with the goods or services anywhere in the world (not necessarily in interstate commerce). Great care should be taken when specifying the date of first use. It is desirable that the specified date of first use be as early a date as possible; the first to use the mark generally wins in any contest of rights. However, error as to the date of first use may sometimes void the registration.

(c) A prescribed number of specimens of the mark as actually used in interstate commerce. Where feasible (such as where the mark is used on labels or tags), actual specimens should be provided. If it is not feasible to provide actual specimens because, *e.g.*, the specimens are unreasonably large or painted directly on the goods, facsimiles must be provided. The facsimiles should be photographic or some other acceptable reproduction, which clearly show the mark and, preferably, how the mark is used on the goods.

The company should also be sure to inform its attorney of any possible concurrent users of which it is aware.

After the application is filed, a Trademark Examiner in the PTO reviews the application to determine whether the mark is, in fact, registerable, that is, capable of distinguishing the applicant's goods from the goods of others. The Examiner also reviews both the Principal and Supplemental trademark registration files maintained at the PTO to determine if the mark is "confusingly similar" to any mark already being used by another. Thus, registering a mark and making it available to the Trademark Examiner tends to prevent registration of confusingly similar marks.

> If a mark survives examination by the PTO, it is published for opposition.

When an application for registration on the Principal Register survives examination, the mark is published in the "Official Gazette" of the PTO.[171] For 30 days after publication, any person who believes that he or she would be damaged by the registration of the mark may file what is known as an "opposition" to registration of the mark.[172] If no opposition is filed at the end of the 30-day period, or if the applicant is successful in withstanding the opposition, a notice of allowance is issued. Oppositions are described in the following section.

[171] 15 U.S.C. §1062(a).
[172] 15 U.S.C. §1063.

If the application was based upon actual use of the mark, the registration is granted in due course. However, if the application was based upon an intent to use, additional procedures are followed. Specifically, a declaration of commencement of use, together with specimens of the use, must be filed by the applicant within six months from the date of the notice of allowance. However, the six-month period can be extended for an additional six months by filing a request for extension together with a verified statement of continued bona fide intention to use the mark and payment of a specified fee. Up to four additional six-month extensions can be obtained upon showing good cause, and payment of additional fees.

After the declaration of commencement of use has been filed, the application is examined a second time. The Examiner considers the specimens filed to ensure that the specimens reflect the same mark and goods described in the applications. Additionally, the Examiner considers any new developments since the first examination, and the possibility of clear error in the first examination. Thus, the second examination will consider such issues as the mark having become generic since the first examination, or relevant prior registrations missed in the first examination.[173]

The use in commerce that must be alleged in the declaration of commencement of use must be the bona fide use of the mark in the ordinary course of trade, and not a token use made merely to reserve a right in the mark. Until the Trademark Law Revision Act of 1988, token sales of a product bearing the mark were sometimes made in an attempt to establish "use" of the mark. It was recognized that such a practice was questionable, but the theory was that a token sale was better than none at all. Therefore, if full dressed commercial sales could not be commenced immediately, a token sale was made in an attempt to establish use, followed as soon as possible by the full dress commercial sales. As of November 16, 1989, token sales are no longer effective to establish actual use. Of course, under the new law, rights can be obtained by filing an application based upon an intent to use.

Once the mark is actually used, and the registration granted, the registrant obtains a nationwide "constructive use" priority, effective as of the date of the application. The constructive use priority provides superior rights to the mark against all other persons except those who (a) used or applied to register the mark prior to the date of the application, or (b) obtained an earlier "effective filing date" by applying to register the mark under Section 44 of the Lanham Act (obtained a priority based upon a filing in a foreign country).[174]

---

[173] 15 U.S.C. §1051(b), (c), (d).
[174] 15 U.S.C. §1057(c).

Contesting Registration: Opposition and Cancellation Proceedings

As previously noted, for a 30-day period after a mark is published, any person who believes that he or she would be damaged by registration of the mark may initiate an "opposition" proceeding to prevent the grant of the registration.[175] An opposition is an *inter partes* proceeding similar to litigation. The opposer is, in effect, in the position of a plaintiff, and the applicant for the registration is in the position of the defendant. The opposer initiates the proceeding by filing a verified (*e.g.*, under oath) opposition paper stating facts which he contends show that the registration should be denied, and that the opposer would be damaged by the issuance of the registration. The grounds for the opposition can be that any of the requisites for the registration are not met, and that the opposer would be damaged by the registration. Typically, the opposer claims that he or she is presently using a mark or trade name which is confusingly similar to the applicant's mark and has been using that mark prior to use of the mark by the applicant. This situation establishes both the requisite damage and the grounds for opposition. The applicant typically counters with an argument that the applicant, in fact, is the prior user, or that there is no likelihood of confusion between the marks, or both. The parties then attempt to prove the facts. A "discovery" period occurs during which written questions (interrogatories) are answered by the parties, specified documents are requested and are produced for the other party to review, and oral depositions are taken. Evidence in the form of exhibits, affidavits, or oral depositions taken before a court reporter are then submitted, together with briefs explaining the parties' positions. An oral argument is then made before the Trademark Trial and Appeal Board, and that Board ultimately renders a decision.

> An opposition is an *inter partes* proceeding similar to litigation.

The trademark laws also provide for a "cancellation" proceeding.[176] The cancellation proceeding is similar to the opposition proceeding and can be brought by any party who believes that he is or will be damaged by the registration of a mark on the Principal Register. The cancellation proceeding is initiated by filing a verified petition stating facts showing the grounds for canceling the mark, and showing that the petitioner will be damaged by continuing the registration. In general, if the cancellation petition is filed within five years after the registration issues, the cancellation proceeding can be based on any ground on which an opposition might have been brought. After five years, however, the cancellation proceeding can be filed only on the basis that: (a) the mark has become a common, descriptive name for the goods; *i.e.*, has become generic; (b) a registrant has abandoned the mark; (c) the registration of the mark was obtained fraudulently; or (d) the

---

[175] 15 U.S.C. §1063; 37 C.F.R. §§2.101-2.106, 2.116-2.135.
[176] 15 U.S.C. §1064; 37 C.F.R. §§2.111-2.115, 2.116-2.135.

registrant is using the mark, or is permitting the mark to be used, to misrepresent the source of goods or services.[177]

Trademark Marking

Once a federal registration has been obtained with respect to a mark, the registrant is entitled to use a registration notice such as an asterisk, or an ® "bug" (typically as a superscript to the mark).

The use of a registration notice or "bug" is not mandatory under the statute. However, the notice or "bug" does provide constructive notice of the registration (obviates the need to prove actual notice of registration when seeking profits or damages against an infringer), and "sets off" the mark. "Setting off" the mark signifies that the term or symbol is intended to be a mark which indicates the source or origin of the goods as opposed to a descriptive term for the goods.

Care must be taken with respect to the use of registration notices. A registration notice is appropriate only when used with the specific term or symbol shown in the registration, and only when the mark is used in connection with goods that are within, or are natural extensions of, the definition of the goods set forth in the registration. Accordingly, when a registered trademark is used in conjunction with a new product, a determination should be made as to whether or not the new product falls within the scope of the definition of goods of the registration. If not, a registration notice should not be used and consideration should be given to filing an application for a new registration.

> Care must be taken to use the ® symbol only with a registered mark in connection with goods defined in the Registration.

It is not necessary that a registration notice accompany each instance or usage of a trademark in a publication or advertising copy. It is sufficient for constructive notice purposes that the registration notice be used prominently at least once in the publication. So long as the notice requirement is met, it is appropriate to use the registration notice only when the mark appears apart from a body of text. Within the body of text, the trademark can generally best be set off by using a distinctive type face.

In circumstances where there is no applicable registration, a ™ symbol is often used to "set off" a mark. The use of the ™ symbol has no legal significance other than to signify that the term or symbol is intended to be a source-identifying trademark.

---

[177] 15 U.S.C. §1064.

Post Registration Actions

Trademark law requires an affidavit of use (referred to as a "Section 8 affidavit") to be filed with the PTO during the fifth year of registration.[178] The affidavit must state that the mark is still in use for at least one of the goods recited in the registration for each of the various classifications of goods. If an affidavit of use is not filed before the beginning of the sixth year, the registration is canceled.

> Unless an affidavit of use is filed during the fifth year of registration, the registration is cancelled.

As previously noted, if a mark is in continuous use for five consecutive years after the date of the registration, and is still in use, an affidavit to that effect can be filed (referred to as a "Section 15 affidavit") to render the mark "incontestable." An "incontestable" status generally strengthens the mark.[179]

Term of the Registration

While trademark protection is of potentially infinite duration, the registration itself must be periodically renewed after each 10-year period. There is no limit on the number of times that the registration can be renewed. The registration is renewed for the next 10-year period by filing the appropriate papers and fees within six months before the expiration of the registration. There is no necessity to file a Section 8 affidavit during the second or further terms of registration. However, when the registration is renewed, it is necessary to indicate that the mark is being used in interstate commerce. In addition, the renewal application must recite only the goods on which the mark is in actual use at that time.

Maintaining Trademark Rights

After rights in a mark are acquired, it is important to prevent the mark from losing its trademark significance. If the mark ceases to distinguish the company's goods or services from those of others, the mark becomes public property and can be used by anyone. In other words, if the primary significance of the mark to the consuming public becomes a descriptor for the nature or characteristics of the goods, rather than an indication of the source of the goods, the mark becomes a common descriptive term and any trademark rights in the mark are lost. Suggested procedures for maintaining trademark rights will be provided in a later section of this handbook.

---

[178] 15 U.S.C. §1058(a).
[179] 15 U.S.C. §1065.

State Anti-Dilution Statutes

Some states have enacted what are known as anti-dilution statutes. Typically, these statutes effectively make any unauthorized use of another's trademark a misdemeanor, resulting in a fine or imprisonment, or create a private right of action to enjoin the unauthorized use. These state statutes, in contradistinction to the federal trademark law, *relate to use on goods which are not the same or similar to goods in connection with which the trademark is used and are limited to trademarks that are so famous that they are recognized as a source indicator even in the absence of a reference to particular goods or services.* For example, if Company Y began selling chewing gum under the mark XEROX, it may be that, since the goods are so dissimilar, the use of the mark on the chewing gum would not be likely to "cause confusion, or to cause mistake or to deceive" the public as to the source of the goods. Accordingly, the use might not be actionable under the federal statute. However, the state anti-dilution statutes are typically not so limited, and the use of a famous mark on the chewing gum would probably be a violation of the state statute. The existence of state anti-dilution statutes must be investigated on a state-to-state basis.

In addition, other bodies of state law and statutes exist, such as the Uniform Deceptive Trade Practices Act, which may be applicable in various situations.

Practical Considerations with Respect to Software Goods

Trademark protection is available for software products in the same manner as for other goods or services. The trademark would be included on packaging, in all documentation, and (where feasible) also in the body of the software in a manner that ensures the trademark is displayed whenever the program is used. Inclusion of the trademark in the body of the program provides a measure of protection against outright copying of the software. If an unauthorized person copies and sells or distributes the software in interstate commerce with the trademark still included in the software, irrespective of other remedies available (*e.g.*, copyright, patent, or trade secret), the very powerful remedies for trademark infringement discussed above may be available.

Use of a trademark does not prevent competitors from copying or reverse engineering a product unless some confusion as to the source or origin of the product is likely. However, distribution of unauthorized copies of software incorporating the trademark can, in many instances, be a trademark infringement. Because of, for example, the lack of quality control of the magnetic media and copying process, and lack of access to support, maintenance, and updates, the unauthorized copy should not be considered to be the goods (or a service) of the trademark owner. Thus, in circumstances where an end user receiving an unauthorized copy including a trademark is likely to think that the source of the copy is the trademark owner, a trademark infringement occurs. Such a likelihood of confusion as to source commonly occurs where the unauthorized copies of the software are obtained for a substantial fee from a commercial establishment in response to a request for the trademark owner's software, particularly if received in the packaging purporting to be that of the trademark owner.

A compelling argument that a likelihood of confusion exists can still be made where the parties to the original unauthorized copying or to distribution of the unauthorized copy were aware that the actual source was not the trademark owner. In many circumstances, potential purchasers of the software who were not party to the original transaction will have access to and use the software. In practice, once software is in the hand of the end user, "back up" copies (disks) of programs are typically used, or the program is installed on a fixed (hard) disk. Accordingly, those persons may well be confused as to the source after viewing the trademark in the displays.

Further market goodwill and recognition of the expertise of the originator (identified by the trademark) tends to give any follow-up or update services provided by the program originator more credence. The availability of follow-up or update services, *i.e.*, access to the expertise of the program originator, tends to enhance the value of authorized, relative to unauthorized, program copies.

Mask Work Protection

Historically, manufacturers and developers of semiconductor chips could not, as a practical matter, prevent competitors from appropriating the substantial investment inherent in developing circuit layout and production masks. None of the classical legal protection mechanisms were effective to protect the developmental aspects of the chip. Notwithstanding the effort and cost of developing a mask, the mask is typically developed by straightforward application of standard engineering principles and generally does not meet the novelty and unobviousness requisites for patentability.[180] Similarly, a mask typically does not constitute a work of authorship under the Copyright Act.[181] Further, as a general proposition, the technology presently available is not cost effective in preventing competing companies from reconstructing and copying the circuit layout and masks associated with the chip once the chip is placed on the market. (The author was privileged to have been one of the persons requested to submit testimony to Congress with respect to the protection of semiconductor products and proposed legislation in that regard.)

A new form of protection for "mask works," *i.e.*, semiconductor chip products, is now available. The new form of protection is, in effect, a hybrid of the copyright and patent protection mechanisms.

---

[180] 35 U.S.C. §§102, 103.
[181] 17 U.S.C. §101, *et seq.*

Protectable Subject Matter; Requisites for Protection

Under the Semiconductor Chip Protection Act (the "Act"), "Mask Works" are defined as a "series of related images, however fixed or enclosed" that represent three dimensional patterns in the layers of a semiconductor chip.[182] Protection is available for any mask work unless:

1. The mask work is not original (that is, the mask work was copied); or

2. The mask work consists of designs that are "staple, commonplace, or familiar in the semiconductor industry, or variations of such design, combined in such a way that, considered as a whole, is not original";[183] or

3. The mask work was first commercially exploited more than two (2) years before the mask work was registered with the Copyright Office.[184]

In order to be eligible for protection, the mask work must also have a nexus to the United States. The owner of the mask work must either be a national or domiciliary of the United States or a foreign country that is party to a treaty with the United States that provides protection of mask works, or a stateless person. However, even if the owner does not fit in any of the above categories, mask work protection is available under the Act if the mask work is first commercially exploited in the United States, or a special presidential proclamation with respect to the owner's country is applicable.[185] The United States nexus provisions were included to encourage other countries to enact similar legislation. A number of countries have now followed suit.[186]

Typically, the owner of a mask work (entitled to protection under the Act) is the person(s) who created the mask work. Presumably, in analogy to the copyright statute, co-creators of the mask work would be co-owners of the mask work protection. However, where the mask work is made within the scope of the creator's employment, the employer is considered the owner of the mask work.[187]

The Act includes various transitional provisions applying to chips that were first commercially exploited prior to the Act, and to protection of mask works by foreign nationals. Under the transitional provisions, protection is available for any

---

[182] The Semiconductor Chip Protection Act of 1984, 17 U.S.C. §901(a)(2).
[183] 17 U.S.C. §902(b).
[184] 17 U.S.C. §908(a).
[185] 17 U.S.C. §902(a).
[186] Generally, analogous laws have been enacted in, for example, Australia, Belgium, Canada, Denmark, Finland, France, Germany, Greece, Ireland, Italy, Japan, Korea, Luxembourg, Netherlands, Norway, Portugal, Spain, Sweden and the United Kingdom.
[187] 17 U.S.C. §901(a)(6).

mask work that was first commercially exploited between July 1, 1983, and the passage of the Act, so long as the mask work was registered with the Copyright Office before July 1, 1985. However, the owner's rights are limited with respect to such chips. Infringing chips manufactured prior to the Act may be imported and/or distributed in the United States until two years after the date of registration upon an offer to pay a reasonable royalty to the mask work owner on the units imported or distributed after the date of the Act.[188] It is not clear exactly how the notice provisions of the Act (to be discussed) interact with the transitional provisions.

> **Mask Work Protection Is Available Unless Mask:**
> - Is not original (copied from another)
> - Consists of staple, commonplace, or familiar designs
> - Was commercially exploited more than two years prior to filing registration
> - Has no U.S. nexus

The transitional provisions also established interim protection for foreign nationals. A petition is made to the Commissioner of Patents and Trademarks for an order extending protection under the Act to nationals of a particular foreign country.[189] Guidelines for submission of applications for interim protection of mask work have been published.[190] In essence, a showing must be made that the foreign country is attempting in good faith to comply with Section 920(a)(1) of the Act.

Scope of Protection

In essence, the Semiconductor Chip Protection Act protects against the use of reproductions of mask works in the manufacture of competing chips. However, the Act makes it absolutely clear that competitors are not precluded from reverse engineering the chip for purposes of analysis[191] or from using any (unpatented) idea, procedure, process, system, method of operation, concept, principle, or discovery embodied in the mask work.[192]

The owner of a protected mask work is provided the exclusive right to reproduce the mask work, and to import and distribute semiconductor chip products in which the mask work is embodied (*i.e.*, chips using layouts according to the mask work).[193] However, the mask work owner's exclusive right is explicitly limited by the so-called "reverse engineering," "first sale (exhaustion of rights)," and "innocent infringer" provisions. The statute effectively limits infringement to instances of commercial exploitation of reproductions of the mask work, *i.e.*, to situations

---

[188] 17 U.S.C. §913.
[189] 17 U.S.C. §914.
[190] 1094 Off. Gaz. Pat. Office 30.
[191] 17 U.S.C. §906(a)(1).
[192] 17 U.S.C. §§902(c), 906(a)(2).
[193] 17 U.S.C. §905.

where competing chips are manufactured using outright copies of the protected mask work. It is permissible under the statute for competitors to reproduce the mask work solely for the purposes of reverse engineering and to use the reverse engineering analysis in the development of the competitor's chip.[194] Thus, competitors are permitted to study a semiconductor chip product, then develop their own corresponding masks (unless precluded by applicable patent rights).

Mask work owners' rights are of necessity limited with respect to importation and sale of unauthorized chips by innocent purchasers of infringing chips. A person who purchases a chip without any reason to believe the chip to be subject to protection (purchases the chip "in good faith and without having notice of protection") is

---

Protected Mask Work

Exclusive Rights:
- Reproducing mask work
- Importing or distributing chip
- Embodying mask work

Limitations:
- Innocent infringement
- Reverse engineering privilege
- First sale

---

considered an innocent purchaser.[195] Where chips are purchased in good faith and without notice, the innocent purchaser does not incur any liability for importing or distributing the chips prior to being given notice that the chip is subject to protection, and is thereafter permitted to dispose of the remainder of the chips upon payment of a "reasonable royalty" on each unit of the infringing chip.[196] However, the innocent purchaser is somewhat at risk with respect to chips that are sold after having been given notice of the protection. Unless the parties agree on a "reasonable royalty," the royalty will be determined by infringement litigation.[197]

The rights of the mask work owner are also limited to a certain extent with respect to the import and sale of authorized chips (chips embodying the mask work made by, or with the permission of, the mask work owner). The owner of the mask work exhausts his rights to control importation and distribution of a particular protected semiconductor chip unit once it is sold. Once the owner of the mask work sells a chip to a third party, the third party is entitled to use the particular unit without the permission of the owner of the mask work. However, the third party does not have the right to reproduce the chip.[198]

---

[194] 17 U.S.C. 906(a).
[195] 17 U.S.C. 901(a)(7), (8).
[196] 17 U.S.C. §907(a), (d).
[197] 17 U.S.C. §907(b).
[198] 17 U.S.C. §906(b).

Notice

The Act provides for constructive notice of mask work protection by use of a "mask work notice" similar to the copyright notice. The use of the mask work notice is not a prerequisite for protection. However, unless the notice is affixed to the semiconductor chips, in an action against an accused infringer it must be proven that the infringer was, or should have been, aware that the mask work was subject to protection. The mask work notice consists of the words "mask work," the symbol *M*, or the symbol Ⓜ, followed by the name of the owner or owners of the mask work.[199]

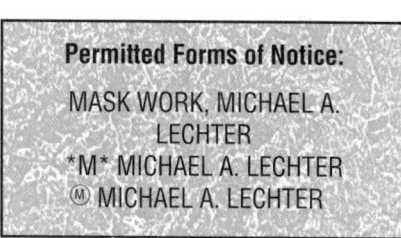

Permitted Forms of Notice:

MASK WORK, MICHAEL A. LECHTER
M MICHAEL A. LECHTER
Ⓜ MICHAEL A. LECHTER

Term; Registration

Under the Act, mask work protection commences upon the first commercial exploitation of the chip (anywhere in the world) or upon registration of the mask work, whichever occurs first. The protection then runs for a term of ten years, expiring at the end of the tenth calendar year.[200] However, in order to maintain mask work protection, the mask work must be registered with the Copyright Office within two years of the first commercial exploitation.[201] Registering a mask work involves the filing of a Copyright Office form together with particular identifying material, and a fee.

Enforcement; Remedies

Registration of a mask work provides a number of very powerful remedies against infringers. Once a registration of the mask work has been obtained (or if registration is applied for and refused, in which case notice must be served on the copyright office), the mask work owner can bring an infringement suit in the federal courts[202] and, if successful, obtain not only injunctive relief and actual damages suffered as a result of the infringement, but also any profits made by the infringer that are not accounted for in the actual damages[203] and, at the court's discretion, all of the costs of the suit, including attorneys' fees.[204] Alternatively, in lieu of actual damages and profits, the owner can obtain an award of statutory damages up to $250,000 (the exact amount is determined by the court).[205] In addition, infringing chips and drawings, layouts and so forth can be impounded or destroyed.[206]

---

[199] 17 U.S.C. §909.
[200] 17 U.S.C. §904.
[201] 17 U.S.C. §908(a).
[202] 17 U.S.C. §910(a); *See also Brooktree Corp. v. Advanced Micro Devices, Inc.*, 10 U.S.P.Q.2d 1374 (S.D. Cal. 1988), *aff'd*, 24 U.S.P.Q.2d 1401 (Fed. Cir. 1992).
[203] 17 U.S.C. §911(a), (b).
[204] 17 U.S.C. §911(f).
[205] 17 U.S.C. §911(c).
[206] 17 U.S.C. §911(e).

The owner of a protected mask work can also prevent importation of infringing chips into the United States. The Treasury Department and Postal Service has issued regulations with respect to exclusion of infringing articles from the United States.[207] It is probable that the regulations will require, as a condition for preventing imported articles from entering the United States, that the protected mask owner either obtain a court order or an order from the International Trade Commission, prove that the mask work is protected and the imported articles are an infringement, and/or post a bond.

Practical Considerations

As a practical matter, the most difficult aspect of enforcing mask work protection is likely to be proving that the accused chip embodies the particular mask work; *i.e.*, the protected mask work was reproduced. The dividing line between infringing reproduction and embodiment of a protected mask work and permitted use of the result of reverse engineering analysis may be a difficult line to draw. Accordingly, mask work developers would be prudent to include "signatures" (*i.e.*, arbitrary, nonfunctional elements) to facilitate proof of copying. Does an infringement occur when the masks used in manufacturing a chip are not actual reproductions of protected mask work, but rather are developed by reproducing the protected mask work and then calling out dimensions to a draftsman on the other side of the room? Arguably, such a practice is merely "incorporating" the results of the analysis or evaluation of the mask work. It remains to be seen how the courts will deal with such situations.

---

[207] 17 U.S.C. §910(c); 19 C.F.R. §12.39(d).

Comparison of the Protection Mechanisms

Each of the respective mechanisms for protecting intellectual property has advantages and disadvantages, as outlined and discussed below. A summary comparison of the term of effectiveness, scope of protection, and other compatible forms of protection, that are available for concurrent use with each mechanism is provided in Appendix I.

A trade secret strategy can provide protection of potentially infinite duration. However, the trade secret is no protection whatsoever against another independently developing the technology, and/or possibly obtaining exclusive proprietary rights to it. For that matter, a trade secret provides no protection against someone copying the technology, as long as he obtains the technology legally and is not under any express or implied contractual obligation not to use the technology.

A trademark provides protection of potentially infinite duration and protects against competition trading on a company's reputation. However, a trademark provides no protection whatsoever against independent development of technology, or, for that matter, copying the technology, so long as there is no likelihood that the public will be confused as to the source or origin of the goods.

Copyright protection, while not potentially infinite, is still of relatively long duration. However, the copyright protects only the form of the expression of an idea, not the substance of an idea. Thus, copyrights provide very limited protection.

Mask work protection is available with respect to semiconductor chip products, but may afford protection only against instances where a reproduction of a mask work is used in the manufacture of competing chips.

A design patent has a term of only 14 years, but provides substantial protection with respect to the ornamental features of a product, that is, the nonfunctional "trade dress" of the product. A design patent, however, does not protect the functional aspects of the product.

A utility patent has a maximum term of only 17 years, but provides the broadest scope of legally available protection. The utility patent can be used to protect the new and unobvious inventive concepts of a product. Of course, in return for this, the details of the product, or at least the details of the product relating to the inventive concepts, must be disclosed to the public. Those details become the property of the public at the end of the 17 years.

The various forms of protection are not necessarily mutually exclusive. In many cases, different forms of protection can be used concurrently with respect to a given product, as summarized in Appendix I.

As a basic proposition, trademark protection can be used in connection with any of the other modes of protection. For example, assume that a company is marketing a hand-held instrument that has a particular ornamental (as opposed to functional) shape. A design patent may be obtained on the ornamental aspects of the casing. At the same time, those ornamental aspects can be used as a trademark. After actual use has commenced, the shape of the casing

---

Combined Protection Strategy for Distinctive Product Appearance/ Ornamental Features

- Obtain design patent
- Begin actual use
- Apply for trademark registration on Supplemental Register
- Explicit mention/emphasis of appearance/feature in advertising/ promotion
- Apply for Principal Registration (presumed distinctive after five years)

can be registered on the Supplemental Register. Moreover, after five continuous years of exclusive use, the secondary meaning is presumed; that is, it is presumed that the shape has become associated with goods originating from the company, and an application for registration on the Principal Register can be made.

In the meantime, the design itself has been protected by the design patent. Also, a utility patent could have been filed on the inventive aspects of the instrument, and if there were particular manufacturing techniques that provided the company a competitive advantage in producing the instrument, but were not related to the actual apparatus, these manufacturing techniques could be maintained as trade secrets without jeopardizing the validity of the patent. However, if a given technique is necessary to make the invention operable, or to make the best mode of the invention, it would necessarily be disclosed in the patent, and thus could not be maintained as a trade secret. Of course, a copyright could be claimed on any documentary material published with respect to the instrument and mask work protection obtained with respect to any custom integrated circuits used.

Combined trade secret and copyright protection also has been attempted. The principal form of protection is a trade secret license, but a copyright notice is included on the distributed materials as secondary protection in the event that the trade secret is lost. However, the inclusion of an effective copyright notice on the product which is being maintained as a trade secret may, in itself, destroy the trade secret. A copyright notice, if it is to be effective, is required to include a date of publication. Thus, the copyright notice can be construed to be an admission that the work has been published, in the copyright sense; *i.e.*, distributed to the public on a nonconfidential basis. Moreover, use of a copyright notice may give rise to a requirement that a copy of the work (or identifying portions thereof in the case of a program) be deposited with the Library of Congress—the very antithesis of secrecy. For this reason, an alternative "provisional" copyright notice in the following form is suggested:

> This is an unpublished work protected by Federal Copyright Law. Unauthorized Reproduction Prohibited. In the event the work is deemed published, the following notice shall apply:
> © MICHAEL A. LECHTER, 1994

Since the "provisional" notice is not a form of notice expressly recognized by the Copyright Act, it is uncertain whether the "provisional" notice will prove adequate. However, as previously discussed, under the 1976 law, publication without a proper copyright notice will not destroy the copyright, so long as registration is made within five years of the publication, and proper remedial measures are taken. Further, works first published after March 1, 1989, require no notice under the Berne Convention.

A sequential trade secret, patent protection strategy may also be employed, where the nature of the product permits. Initially (preferably after a patent application is filed on the product), the product may be marketed under "trade secret" licenses. Since the patent application is maintained in secrecy by the Patent and Trademark Office until the patent grant is actually issued, no conflict arises between the modes of protection. In fact, the effectiveness of a license is often bolstered by the inhibiting effect of a "patent pending" notice on would-be copiers. If no patent is ultimately issued, the Patent Office files are never opened to the public (except in particular special circumstances), so that the trade secret can be maintained. If a patent issues, the license would still be effective, defining the rights licensed under the patents.

Concurrent use of the patent and trade secret mechanisms can also sometimes be used to protect different aspects of a product. Such interaction, however, must be carefully considered. An application for a patent must include a detailed description of the "best mode" of the invention known to the inventor at the time the application is filed.[208] Certainly, any element or feature that is necessary to the operation of the invention or that makes the invention practical must be disclosed (and presumably should be claimed) in the patent application. Further, it has been argued that the application should include all major details relating to the invention known to the inventor at the time the application is filed, to comply with the requirement that the application describe the "best mode" of the invention. In the case of an inventive algorithm, such details could exclude the data manipulation techniques, and perhaps specific code, used in implementation.

On the other hand, the inventor is not required to (and, in fact, is prohibited from) adding new descriptive matter to a patent application after filing. Accordingly, details developed after filing the application legitimately may be either the subject of another patent application or maintained as a trade secret.[209] For this reason, it is sometimes advisable to file a patent application at an early stage of development of a product. However, it is imperative to thoroughly review the patent application as the commercial embodiment is developed to ensure that all operationally necessary details are described in the application and that the claims provide proper coverage. If a review is not timely made, it is possible that intervening publications or sales will ultimately bar obtaining patent protection.

---

[208] 35 U.S.C. §112.
[209] See, e.g., 35 U.S.C. §120.

In developing a protection strategy for a software product, consideration should be given to such issues as the difficulty in adapting the software to different hardware systems, and the medium of distribution (e.g., source code, object code, magnetic disc, cassette, ROM, PROM), the cost and volume of the products to be protected, the amount of administration that is acceptable, and the intended markets.

Thus, with a little bit of forethought, an appropriate strategy using each of the various protection mechanisms to its best effect can be developed to protect a given product. The particular approach to protecting a given product must be tailored to the specific characteristics and form of the product as marketed, as well as the specific marketing approach and distribution scheme contemplated.

Suggested Procedures

It is imperative that policies and procedures be implemented to ensure that intellectual property assets are maximized and potential liabilities are minimized. Any procedures adopted by a company must be tailored to the particulars of that company. However, the following guidelines are provided for general reference. A sample procedure statement is provided in Appendix II.

Securing and Maintaining Rights in Technology

Employee Non-Disclosure and Non-Use Agreements

In general, an "employee" agreement should be obtained from each employee that may have access to confidential information (*e.g.*, proprietary know-how) or is in a position likely to generate technology. The agreement should impose an obligation of confidentiality (non-disclosure and non-use) on the employee with respect to confidential information, and require the employee to assign to the company rights to any works of authorship and technology developed by the employee that relate to the company's business.

Preliminary State of the Art Investigation

At the beginning of each new project or entry into a new field of endeavor, a preliminary investigation of the state of the art, and, in particular, issued patents should be conducted. This will provide an idea of the patents already held by others in the relevant area of technology, and can help identify potential infringement problems. It can also provide a starting point for research.

Initially Keep R & D as a Trade Secret

Initially, all R & D should be maintained as a trade secret. Appropriate non-disclosure (confidentiality) agreements should be obtained from all third parties given access to confidential information (vendors and consultants and the like). Preferably, the agreements will also make it clear that all technology that is developed by the consultant or vendor during a project will be assigned to the company.

Maintain Documentation

Proper records relating to the developmental process should be maintained. The records should establish conception, reduction to practice, and diligence in reducing the invention to practice after conceiving it. The more information and documentation that can be shown, the more likely that the requisite conception, reduction to practice, and diligence for an early date of invention in the United States can be established. Detailed records of the development process can also be critical to defending against third party claims of

> Keep records sufficient to establish the date of invention.

trade secret, copyright, and mask work infringement. The necessity of keeping records and more particular suggested procedures will be discussed later in this handbook.

Timely Consideration of Patent Protection

The prospect of patent protection should be explored for each aspect or feature of a product that provides a competitive advantage in a marketplace. It is important to keep the potential consequences in mind when considering whether to show a product or offer it for sale. A patentability assessment should be performed, and patent applications filed, if appropriate, before any public use or showing, publication, or offer for sale.

> Keep the potential bars to patent in mind.

A patent disclosure should be generated. In general, the disclosure should be as complete as possible, and it should identify anything that might be relevant to the issue of patentability and any possible public uses or offers for sale. Drafting the disclosure can be facilitated by adopting an appropriate form. If earlier searches do not make it unnecessary, patentability investigations of particular features of a product should be conducted.

To ensure timely consideration of patent issues, it is sometimes desirable to establish a systematic procedure involving periodic meetings of a patent committee, or periodic meetings between the engineers and a designated patent liaison or attorney. Any procedure established must be tailored to the particular company. An exemplary statement of procedures for a large multi-national company is included as Appendix II.

Infringement Clearance Procedure

Before any product is placed on the market, potentially applicable third party intellectual property rights should be investigated and analyzed. The various preliminary searches noted above should identify potential infringement problems relatively early on. However, it is sometimes prudent to do additional searching, *i.e.*, when additional features are added to the product after, or perhaps as a result of, the earlier searches.

> Potential infringement problems cannot be ignored.

If a potential infringement problem is identified, it cannot be ignored. Even if the company's employees are convinced in their own minds that there is in fact no infringement, it still may be necessary to have a formal attorney's invalidity/non-infringement opinion in the file, just in case. If a company is found to infringe a patent of which it is aware, and did not obtain the opinion of a competent patent attorney, the infringement will be considered willful, and the company could be liable for treble damages and the patentee's attorney's fees.

Keeping Accurate Records

Need For Keeping Accurate Records

There are a number of instances when it becomes necessary to prove the date and nature of technical activities, and the project with which the activities are associated. For example, such proofs are often determinative in:

> Disputes regarding ownership of technology—whether certain technology was first made under a particular "development" contract or Government contract;

> Disputes regarding whether particular technology is covered by a particular license agreement;

Disputes regarding whether certain technology is subject to a confidentiality or non-use agreement;

Proving an invention was previously developed, not abandoned, suppressed, or concealed, as a defense to patent infringement under 35 U.S.C. §102(g); and

Interference proceedings before the PTO—contests to determine "priority of invention."

Development and Government Contracts

"Development" agreements often specify that a particular party will obtain rights (*e.g.*, title or a license to make, use, and sell) to all technology "arising from work done under the contract" or "first conceived or first made under the contract." Where the company is in the position of a developer under such contracts, it is imperative to be able to show that:

(1) certain technology was created prior to the contract; and

(2) certain technology that was developed on other projects during the term of the agreement was, in fact, developed on those other projects.

Where the preexisting technology can be identified beforehand, *e.g.*, when there are preexisting patents or patent applications, it is best to expressly except (obtain a waiver with respect to) such technology. However, preexisting technology not anticipated to be relevant to a project frequently turns out to be relevant to the project after the fact. In this case, rights to the technology often turn on the ability to prove that the technology was, in fact preexisting.

Similar circumstances arise with respect to technology being developed in connection with projects concurrent with, but separate from, work done under the agreement. Rights to technology that would otherwise be held by the company can be lost if records clearly differentiating work done on the respective projects have not been conscientiously and accurately maintained.

License Agreements

In general, it is desirable that license agreements clearly and concisely particularize the licensed technology. However, certain license agreements (typically entered into in settlement of a dispute) sometimes relate to all technology "made prior to the date of the agreement." It then becomes imperative to be able to prove, after the fact, when technology was "made" vis-a-vis the date of the agreement. The ability to do this, however, typically turns on the sufficiency of the records that were generated contemporaneously with the technology.

Confidentiality and Non-Use Agreements

Confidentiality and non-use agreements are often entered into in connection with various business negotiations. Such agreements often include provisions to the effect that technology which:

(a) was already in the possession of the company; or

(b) is independently developed by the company

are *not* subject to the confidentiality and non-use provisions. It is generally incumbent on the recipient of information, however, to prove "prior possession" or "independent development." Thus, records that show the history of the development of the technology (when specific acts occurred and the particular individuals involved in those acts) should be maintained contemporaneously with the development.

Prior Development Defense to Patent Infringement and Interference Proceedings

As previously discussed, the U.S. patent statute requires that, in order to obtain a patent, an applicant must be the first to have "made" the invention in the United States. The statute states:

> §102 A person shall be entitled to a patent unless—
> . . . .
> (g) before the applicant's invention thereof, the invention was made *in this country* by another who had not abandoned, suppressed, or concealed it. In determining priority of invention, there shall be considered not only the respective dates of conception and reduction to practice of the invention, but also the reasonable diligence of one who was first to conceive and last to reduce to practice, from a time prior to conception by the other.

The situation sometimes arises where two different inventors develop the same invention independently. In such a case, only the first to have "made" the invention in the United States, who did not abandon, suppress, or conceal the invention, is entitled to the patent. If only the second party to "make" the invention files an application which ultimately issues as a patent, and that patent is asserted against the first to have made the invention, "prior development" is a defense against the charge of infringement (assuming no abandonment, suppression, or concealment, *e.g.*, assuming the technology was not maintained as a trade secret). If both parties file patent applications, the relative priority of the inventors is determined by an "interference" proceeding conducted by the PTO as previously discussed.

The Two-Step Process of "Making an Invention"

As previously discussed, "making" an invention, as that term is used in the statute (and is typically used in the agreements mentioned above), is a two-step process:

(a) *conceiving* the invention (technology); then

(b) reducing the invention to practice.

"Conception" is basically the mental portion of the inventive act. "Reducing the invention to practice" is, in basic terms, building the invention and proving that it works for its intended purpose. The filing of a patent application is considered to be a "constructive" reduction to practice.

With respect to 35 U.S.C. §102(g), the diligence with which the company works, after the technology has been conceived, to reduce the technology to practice is also a factor. As a general proposition, if inventor A was both the first to conceive and the first to reduce the invention to practice, inventor A will be deemed the first to have "made" the invention. Further, if the first to conceive the invention, but the last to reduce the invention to practice, inventor A will still be deemed first to have made the invention if *"diligence"* in pursuing the reduction to practice from a time period prior to the conception of the invention by inventor B can be proven. However, if inventor A cannot prove reasonable diligence in pursuing the reduction to practice beginning with a date before inventor B conceived the invention, inventor B will be deemed first to have made the invention.

Record Keeping Procedures

Record keeping was discussed briefly in connection with the "First to Make the Invention" requirement of the patent law. As a general proposition, *each aspect of the two-step process of making an invention must occur in (or be transported into) the United States and must be proven by more than just the word of the inventor;* the word of the "inventor" (or even co-inventors) as to when and where an invention was conceived or reduced to practice is essentially worthless without "corroboration." Corroboration can be in the form of dated documents, drawings, time records, and oral testimony by "non-inventors."

Preliminary Concept Report Form

Positive proof of a conception date in the United States can be assured by the procedure of filing a Preliminary Concept Report with a designated company official (**in the United States**) or U.S. attorney when an invention is conceived. The Concept Report should fully describe the invention, and, to the extent possible, be signed and dated by the inventors, and ultimately be witnessed (read, signed, and dated) by the receiving company official or attorney.

Search Request and Invention Disclosure Forms sent to the designated company official or U.S. attorney can also be employed to provide proof of conception in the United States. (Exemplary forms provided in Appendices III and IV.)

Notebooks

As a practical matter, however, invention disclosure forms typically do not contain the detail necessary to prove actual reduction to practice of an invention or "diligence." For this reason, *detailed contemporaneous laboratory notebooks should be maintained.* The value of an entry in a laboratory notebook as proof of diligence and/or reduction to practice of an invention is directly proportional to the specificity of the entry and the care which was taken to date and sign each entry and have each entry read, signed and dated by a witness. The following guidelines for keeping notebooks are offered:

> The evidentiary value of records must be considered.

1. All engineers should maintain a *bound* engineering notebook. The context of the entry in an engineering notebook can sometimes be used to prove a date. For example, if an entry showing conception is found in a *bound* engineering notebook, between entries dated the 3rd of January and the 5th of January, it is relevant proof that the invention was conceived sometime between the 3rd and 5th of January. It would not be so relevant, however, if a looseleaf engineering notebook had been used. Blank portions of pages should be lined through.

2. Every entry should be signed and dated, indicate the particular project with which the entry is associated, and, if possible, be signed and dated by a "witness." It is often advantageous to include a "header" on each notebook entry:

> DATE: _____
> PROJECT NO.: _____
> SUBJECT: _____
> SIGNATURE: _____
> WITNESSES: _____

To facilitate such a "header," stamps for printing the header can be issued to each person keeping a notebook.

3. All computations, circuit diagrams, test results, etc., should be *contemporaneously* entered *into the notebook*. It is as easy to do calculations, etc., in the notebook as on scratch paper. So long as the entry is legible (and contains sufficient detail), there are no particular format or "neatness" requirements.

4. It is, however, imperative that each notebook entry identify the subject of the work with *particularity* and contain all relevant details. An entry such as "work on new sharpener" sheds little light on whether the "new sharpener" included a specific feature on a particular date.

5. All persons involved in the work should be identified in the corresponding notebook entries. Unless participants are identified, it is often difficult to establish, long after the fact, those involved in particular activities.

6. It is especially important that all loose papers, such as blue prints, schematics, flow charts, strip charts, oscillographs, photographs of models, etc., be signed and dated, cross-referenced to a particular notebook entry, and, preferably, mounted (taped or stapled) in the body of the appropriate notebook entry. Similarly, physical results of tests, such as samples, models, prototypes, and the like, should be carefully labeled with the date, cross-referenced to notebook entries and retained.

7. Notebooks and records should be maintained in contemplation of proving not only the dates of conception and reduction to practice, but also diligence in between. To this end, it is desirable to have the documentary evidence and, in particular, dated notebook entries describe *all* testing performed, the particular types of equipment used, and the results of the testing, both good *and bad*.

8. A hard copy, or write-once-read-many-times (worm) copy, of each iteration of computer programs should be generated, signed, dated, and witnessed (or a signed dated log maintained with respect to the worm copy). Magnetic media or other alterable media provide much less evidentiary support for establishing a date.

Time Records

Time records, if carefully and accurately maintained with a sufficiently high level of discrimination between respective projects, can also be used to prove, for example, "diligence," "independent development," and that certain technology was not made under a given contract. To make use of time records to these ends, of course, separate project numbers must be assigned to specific, relatively narrowly defined tasks.

Conclusion

In all, a documentary record should be maintained that is capable of establishing the dates and activities comprising each of the elements of "making" an invention, identifying individuals involved in the work who can provide testimonial proof, and identifying the particular project with which technical work is associated.

Securing and Maintaining Rights in Trademarks

Choice of a Mark

As previously discussed, a mark is categorized by its primary meaning to an educated consumer—a consumer who is aware of the goods of the type at issue, and a potential purchaser of the goods. The less descriptive the mark, the more protectable it is. Basically, the strongest and most protectable mark is a simple, arbitrary symbol or design, or a relatively euphonious and easily pronounced coined word. Of course, marketplace considerations may dictate that a term of a more descriptive nature be used.

Use the Mark as a Source Indicator

The consumer's understanding of a term can be shaped by the manner in which the term is used. The manner in which a mark is used in advertising, promotional materials, and internal and external correspondence can be the determinative factor in this regard. If a perfectly good mark is used as a descriptor or a generic term, it will ultimately come to be understood as a generic or descriptive term and will cease to be protectable.

> The manner in which a mark is used may largely determine the viability of the mark.

Consider an accused infringer's argument:

> "Your Honor, even in their own advertising the word is used as a descriptive, in fact generic, term. Certainly my client is entitled to do the same."

On the other hand, any term, packaging, configuration, or anything that is not clearly generic, can be transformed into a protectable trademark through the manner in which it is used in advertising. For example:

> "Look for the distinctive orange handle!"

> "If you see the big blue stripe, you know it's from Clientco, and you know it's good."

General Rules

Some general rules for using trademarks in advertising and promotional material are as follows:

1. *USE THE MARK ONLY AS A SOURCE INDICATOR.*
   Except to refer to the company where the trademark is also the company name, the company should take care that neither it, nor others, uses the trademark in other than a trademark sense, that is, other than to designate the company as the source or origin of the goods. A trademark should never be used in a manner which tends to designate (name) or describe the type or characteristics of the goods with which the mark is used. Except

   > A trademark must indicate source – never use a trademark as a noun.

when properly used as a company name, a trademark or service mark should never be used as a shorthand name for the goods, as a noun, hyphenated with another word, as a verb, or in a possessive sense. All too often an aggressive marketer intentionally, through its own advertising and promotional activities, causes a trademark to become synonymous with the goods, and thus unwittingly squanders the sales value of the trademark. To prevent use of the mark as a noun, always follow the mark with a specific descriptive generic term for the product. The generic term must provide a satisfactory substitute as the type descriptor for the product. In practice, where the generic term does not adequately indicate the nature of the product, the trademark tends to be employed to serve that function and ultimately becomes genericized. In fact, when a product is the first of its kind, a trademark owner may have to invent not only a source identifier mark, but also a descriptor for the type of a product. Sometimes when a product is the first of its kind, not only must a source identifier mark be invented, but also a descriptor for the type of product. For example:

"The Xerox **photocopier**"; not "The Xerox machine."

The term "machine" is, in effect, too generic. It is not sufficiently descriptive to tell the consumer the nature of the product.

2. *THE TRADEMARK NATURE OF A TERM OR SYMBOL SHOULD ALSO BE MADE CLEAR BY THE MANNER IN WHICH THE MARK IS USED.* The mark should always be used in conjunction with a descriptive term or name for the goods. The trademark should, however, be "set off" from the description or name of the goods. This can be done with distinctive fonts, color, quotation marks, capitalization, or the ™ or, if registered, ® symbol. Some form of trademark notice such as a statement that the mark is a trademark of the company or is registered in the U.S. Patent and Trademark Office should also be used as appropriate. However, it should be noted that setting off a mark, or using a registration notice, while a mitigating factor, will not cure an impropriety in the use of the mark.

3. *DO NOT USE THE MARK IN A CONTEXT WHICH DETRACTS FROM THE TRADEMARK SIGNIFICANCE OF THE TERM.* For example, it is typically not appropriate to use a string of consecutive trademarks in relation to a single descriptive term for the goods. In such a case, it could be argued that only one of the terms was being used as a trademark and the others were merely descriptive terms designating a particular type of goods. For the same reason, a mark should not be preceded by the corporate name.

4. *THE MARK SHOULD BE USED IN THE SAME FORM THAT IT IS REGISTERED.*

5. *EMPHASIZE THE MARK TO THE CONSUMER.* To the extent possible, advertisements and promotional materials should specifically call the consumer's attention to the mark. This is particularly true if the mark is other than a wordmark. Such emphasis will bolster, if not create, rights in the mark.

6. *MONITOR THE USE OF THE MARK.* Use of the trademark by others, as well as by the company itself, should be monitored to guard against misuse. Unauthorized or uncontrolled use of the mark by others can result in the mark becoming generic or being deemed abandoned. The marketplace should be regularly monitored for use of a similar mark that is likely to cause confusion among customers, and the Office Gazette of the PTO should be systematically reviewed against attempts by competitors to register similar marks for use with similar products. Also, publications where the term might appear other than in a context of a company-generated text should be reviewed on a systematic basis, and prompt action taken in the event that a misuse is discovered. Typically, the misuse is inadvertent, and publishers tend to cooperate once advised of a misuse.

7. *MAINTAIN STRICT CONTROL OF USE.* Any authorized use by third parties must be stringently controlled. Quality control must be exercised over all goods or services with which the mark is used, or the mark is at risk of being deemed abandoned.

Procedures for Avoiding Potential Infringement of Third-Party Intellectual Property Rights

In theory, the basic rule with respect to using or copying an aspect of a competitor's product is simple: absent an express or implied contractual obligation, a company is at liberty to use and copy any unpatented, uncopyrighted aspect that comes into a company's possession legally, as long as there is no likelihood that the public would be deceived or confused as to the source of a product.

Practice, however, is another story. The incidence and outcome of intellectual property litigation is often a function of the internal procedures of the contestants.

Avoiding Infringement of Third Party Trade Secret Rights

The analysis in determining whether any given information or technology constitutes a trade secret or is confidential is inevitably a fact-specific inquiry. Nonetheless, it is without question that a competitor's trade secret rights cannot prevent the company from independently developing information or technology or, for that matter, using or copying information or technology, if it is obtained legally and the company is not under any express or implied contractual obligation to the contrary.

By way of preventative procedures, any competitor's materials that come into a company's possession should be reviewed for proprietary notices. While in many instances such material is in fact not "confidential" due to lack of controls by the competitor, prudence may dictate discarding such materials. In addition, in an abundance of caution, the following procedures might be adopted:

1. Promulgate a policy statement directing employees not to use any potentially trade secret information (or at least to consult counsel prior to using).

2. Any new hire that was formerly an employee of a competitor should be debriefed, and it should be made clear that the company is not interested in using any confidential information regarding the new hire's previous employer that the new hire might have.

3. Detailed records of the development of products should be maintained to prove that any potentially trade secret information that might have been acquired from a competitor was not incorporated in a company's products.

Avoiding Infringement of Third Party Patents

It is also possible that a competitor holds utility patents covering new and unobvious aspects of its products, or design patents covering the appearance of its products. The scope of a utility patent is defined by the patent claims; a patent is infringed if an unlicensed product includes the equivalent of each and every element of any of the patent claims. Infringement exists even if the product has additional features or elements that are not included in the claim and even if those additional elements are in themselves patentable. In essence, a design patent is infringed if an unlicensed product is so similar in appearance to the patented design that a consumer, under normal market conditions, is likely to think them the same. Neither patented invention nor design need be actually copied from the patent or competitor's product for infringement to exist; independent development is no defense.

Since independent development is no defense to patent infringement, the following preventative procedures are suggested:

1. Prior to entering into any new product area, or initiating development of significant new features or aspects of a product, have a preliminary investigation performed to collect copies of any relevant patents.

2. Initiate an investigation of all known competitors to obtain copies of any patents they may hold.

3. Examine competitors' products for patent markings or reference to pending applications.

4. Maintain a continuing watch for patents issued to major competitors.

5. Consider having an extensive infringement investigation performed prior to introducing a significant new product. (A cost-benefit analysis should be performed in view of previous searching and knowledge of extant patents.)

6. Develop the company's own portfolio of patents for cross-licensing in the event that the claims of a competitor's patent cannot be, or for some reason are not, avoided.

Avoiding Infringement of Third Party Copyrights

It is prudent to assume that a competitor holds a copyright on all of its "works of authorship," such as booklets, advertising brochures, artistic designs, maps and architectural blueprints, audio tapes and records, and, at least to some extent, computer programs. However, copyright protection is of particularly limited scope: copyright protection pertains only to the form of expression and not to substance (ideas, methods, systems, mathematical principles, formulas, and equations are expressly not copyrightable); and actual copying is a requisite element for infringement (independent development is a defense).

While independent development is a complete defense to a charge of copyright infringement, copying is presumed from "access" and "substantial similarity." Unfortunately, there is a line of cases which have, through some leap of logic, assumed access merely by virtue of the fact that the copyrighted work was available in the marketplace, where there was substantial similarity. Where software is concerned, this can be problematical. Practical and functional reasons sometimes dictate a particular approach; indeed, there are optimum ways of programming toward which competent programmers independently gravitate. In addition, various conventions with respect to, for example, labeling instructions and naming variables have been adopted throughout the industry. In view of these circumstances, it is prudent that the development process be documented in depth so that the company will be able to prove that the work was in fact independently developed.

A company must also beware of the use of unauthorized copies of software in the workplace by its employees. The company may be liable for copyright infringement because of its employees' actions. A policy statement forbidding use of unauthorized copies of software should be issued. It is also prudent to keep records of the acquisition of software on an ongoing basis.

Avoiding Infringement of Third Party Trademark Rights

A trademark (or service mark) is anything that identifies the source or origin of a product (or service), that is, distinguishes the goods or services of one company from those of another. It must be appreciated that a competitor can acquire trademark rights not only in logos and brand names, but also in such things as trade dress (*e.g.*, package design), arbitrary color schemes, and in some instances, even the smell of a product. Rights in a trademark can be acquired through actual use of the mark with goods or services in commercial transactions, or by filing an application for trademark registration based upon a bona fide intent to use. (It is as if use of the mark began on the date of the application.) In general, the first to use a given mark in connection with particular goods in a given geographical area, obtains the rights to the mark for use with those goods in that area. Federal registration prevents someone in a geographical area where the mark is not currently being used from subsequently obtaining rights in the mark.

In a manner of speaking, a trademark protects the market value of the company's reputation and goodwill, as well as protecting investments in advertising and other promotional activities used to develop goodwill. Under the law, a competitor is prevented from effectively capitalizing on a trademark owner's reputation and goodwill by passing off its goods as those made or sponsored by the trademark owner or otherwise creating, intentionally or unintentionally, a likelihood that consumers might be misled or confused as to sponsorship by, or affiliation with, the trademark owner.

However, a competitor's trademark does not preclude independent development of technology or, for that matter, copying the technology, so long as there is no likelihood that the public will be confused as to the source or origin of the goods or sponsorship or affiliation with the trademark owner. Potential trademark infringements can be avoided by timely investigations prior to adopting a trademark.

Avoiding Infringement of Third Party Mask Work Registrations

To the extent that any product that a company might ultimately develop includes custom semiconductor chips, third party "mask work" protection may be applicable. As previously noted, a mask work registration, in essence, precludes the use of reproductions of the protected mask work to manufacture competing chips. However, the act protects only against outright copying, and expressly permits reverse engineering the chip for purposes of analysis and using any unpatented idea, principle, or technology embodied in the mask work.

Thus, as in the case of copyrights, independent development of mask work technologies is a complete defense and, as a matter of procedure, development should be fully documented.

Overview and Comparison of Agreements Affecting Intellectual Property Rights and Liabilities

Rights in intellectual property are often affected, and liabilities created, by various types of agreements. Obviously, this includes agreements specifically related to the transfer of rights (assignment, licenses, franchises, and technical assistance). However, certain other types of agreements, while not for the specific purpose of affecting intellectual property rights, may well affect intellectual property rights or create potential liabilities. Those agreements tend to relate to three broad categories of subject matter: internal relationships (employee, and non-competition); third party business relationships (confidentiality, consulting, development, maintenance and support, manufacturing, and joint venture); and sales and market relationships (purchase, distribution, VAR, and OEM).

Brief descriptions of the more common examples of such agreements and the intellectual property issues most often encountered in such agreements are provided.

Agreements Regarding Transfers of Rights

Assignments, licenses, and technical assistance agreements (and sometimes joint ventures), directly affect rights in intellectual property; all are vehicles for transferring or granting rights in intellectual property to an entity.

Assignments

An assignment is a document that effects a present transfer of title to, for example, various intellectual property rights. In most instances, to be effective with respect to a patent, copyright, or trademark, an assignment must be recorded with the Patent and Trademark or Copyright Office. In general, there should be a recorded assignment with respect to each patent owned by the company, and with respect to each copyright or trademark acquired from outside of the company.[210]

Where the assignment pertains to an invention, the document typically should cover both rights in the United States and throughout the world, including any rights or priorities under international treaties. The assignment should also cover any continuing applications. The document should also include a provision requiring the assignee to execute any papers necessary to perfect the assignor's rights.

License Agreements: In General

A license agreement is, in general terms, an agreement whereby the "licensor," for an agreed upon consideration, grants to the "licensee" certain rights with respect to intellectual property of the licensor. A license is to be distinguished from a sale or an assignment. A sale or assignment transfers substantially all commercial rights and title to the intellectual property to the assignee. In the case of a license, the licensor retains title to the intellectual property.

There are a number of reasons why a company would be willing to permit others to use its intellectual property. Some of these reasons, such as obtaining a royalty income in consideration for use of the intellectual property, are obvious. This is particularly so where the licensor does not itself use the technology; or the licensor is unable or unwilling to meet the demand for products using the intellectual property itself. For example, the licensor may not have the capital to expand its production facilities. The licensor may have other product lines to which it must devote all of its resources. For various reasons, it may not be practical or economical for a company to export product into a particular geographic area, or to establish its own manufacturing facilities in that area. In some cases, the licensor does not have the resources or contacts to develop a necessary distribution system in the area.

There are additional reasons for licensing intellectual property, however, that are not necessarily obvious. For example, having an additional source for a given product may increase the market acceptance of the product. In other instances, the licensor itself might use the licensed product as a part in another product, or sell the licensed product as part of an overall line of products, but find it uneconomical or impractical to manufacture the licensed product itself. By licensing another party that can economically manufacture the product, the licensor can ensure

---

[210] See 35 U.S.C. §261; 15 U.S.C. §1060; 17 U.S.C. §§204, 205.

a source of supply. The fact that the product may also be available to the licensor's competitors is offset by the compensation paid to the licensor by the licensee.

In other instances, licensing a local entity in a given geographic area to manufacture one product may create a market in that geographical area, or at least increase market acceptance, for other products of the licensor.

All license agreements should include certain basic elements. In the most general of terms, for a license agreement to be enforceable, the agreement must: somehow identify, or be attributable to, respective legal entities with the capacity to enter the agreement; include some manifestation of assent by the parties; reflect some manner of consideration between the parties (in some cases a specific recitation of consideration is required); and include terms which are not illegal or otherwise unenforceable under the applicable law.

The typical license agreement includes a number of major sections:

1. A preamble which identifies the parties;

2. A set of recitals which, in effect, describe the background understandings of the agreement of the parties;

3. A recital of consideration, where necessary;

4. Provisions relating to the grant of rights and ownership to intellectual property and confidentiality;

5. Provisions relating to performance by the parties;

6. Provisions relating to the consideration to be paid;

7. Provisions relating to representations and warranties by the parties;

8. Provisions relating to the term and termination of the agreement;

9. Various miscellaneous provisions; and

10. Signatures and acknowledgements.

If the agreement is well written, it will also include definitions for every significant term in the agreement that could conceivably be misunderstood. The definitions are typically included as a separate section at the beginning of the agreement. However, the definitions are also sometimes provided in the body of the agreement, as the terms are introduced in context.

Patent Licenses

A patent license is an agreement under which the "licensor," for an agreed-upon consideration, agrees not to interfere with the performance of some act by the "licensee" that the licensee would otherwise be precluded from doing by the licensor's patent. In the broadest sense, the licensor agrees not to enforce the patent against the licensee with respect to certain acts by the licensee, typically making, using, or selling processes or products covered by the patent. The patent license typically permits the licensee to use, or manufacture and sell, the patented product while at the same time protecting the licensee from competition. Non-licensed third parties are not permitted to manufacture the product.

A patent license may be no more than a covenant not to enforce the patent, or may be coupled with an agreement providing the transfer of know-how or technical assistance. Essentially all countries that have patent systems in place recognize patent licenses.

Know-How Licenses

A know-how license is an agreement whereby the licensor, for an agreed-upon consideration, permits the licensee to have access to, and use, the licensor's know-how. The know-how may be proprietary or non-proprietary. If proprietary know-how is involved, significant features of the license agreement are provisions requiring the licensee to maintain the know-how in confidence (non-disclosure provisions), and, typically, provisions restricting the manner in which the know-how can be used. Such provisions are necessary to protect the licensor's proprietary interest in the know-how.

Trademark Licenses

A trademark license is an agreement under which the owner of a trademark, for an agreed consideration, permits another entity to employ the trademark in connection with the other entity's goods or services. In practice, a trademark license permits the licensee to take advantage of the goodwill associated with the trademark. At the same time, the licensor is able to expand its goodwill through, and, of course, make money from, the licensee's efforts. Trademark licensing is recognized under the laws of most, but not all, countries. In most instances, however, in order for the trademark owner to retain rights in the mark, the trademark owner must maintain careful quality control over the products of the licensee.

When is a trademark license necessary to maintain the trademark owner's rights in a mark? As a general proposition, a merchant or dealer that merely resells bona fide goods bearing a trademark, without changing those goods, does not require a trademark license, as long as the dealer is not holding itself to be authorized or otherwise sponsored by or associated with the trademark owner. A trademark license is necessary when an entity other than the trademark owner is manufacturing goods and using the trademark in connection with those goods.

Franchise Agreements

A franchise agreement can be considered a species of license agreement that grants particularly significant rights and establishes a close, ongoing relationship between the transferor and transferee. Very often the franchise agreement involves a trademark license, together with agreements as to know-how and technical assistance, as well as a license under any applicable patents. Franchise agreements are closely regulated throughout the United States and in many countries.

Technical Services and Assistance Agreements

There are no standard definitions for the terms "technical assistance agreement" or "technical services agreement." In general, however, these are hybrid consulting-know-how agreements relating to provisions of know-how, instruction, and training to the receiving party. Proprietary or non-proprietary know-how, or both, may be involved. For example, an entity with special expertise may be engaged to assist in implementing or installing an equipment plant or process, and to instruct and train the contracting party in the operation and management of the plant or process. The plant, process or equipment may have been acquired from a consultant, or, may have been acquired from a third party, and the consultant is merely engaged to install the equipment and train the other party in its use.

Hybrid License Agreements

A given licensing agreement can pertain to any number of types of intellectual property. For example, a single agreement can grant rights with respect to patents, existing proprietary know-how (trade secret) rights, existing non-proprietary know-how, rights to use certain trademarks and/or trade dress, and the rights to future intellectual property acquired by the licensor.

Where patents covering the subject matter of a license agreement exist, the agreement normally will include a grant of some manner of rights under the patent; rights to use know-how may be worthless if the only practical use to which the know-how can be put is precluded by an applicable patent.

A know-how or technical assistance or service agreement is typically employed when there are no applicable patents, and may sometimes be used in conjunction with a trademark license or franchising agreement.

Where both patents and know-how are involved in a transaction, the grants with respect to both patents and know-how are typically included in a single agreement. The typical practice with respect to trademarks, however, is to have a separate trademark license agreement, even if patents or know-how are also being licensed as part of the overall arrangement. The exception to this practice is where know-how is transferred to facilitate the quality control provisions of the trademark license agreement.

Agreements Regarding Internal Relationships

Agreements with employees are often essential to obtaining and maintaining rights in intellectual property.

Employee Agreements as to Confidentiality and Ownership of Intellectual Property

In general, from a company's perspective, each employee that may have access to confidential information (*e.g.*, proprietary know-how) should be the signatory of an agreement imposing an obligation of confidentiality (non-disclosure and non-use) on the employee with respect to confidential information. The agreement should also require the employee to assign to the company all rights to any works of authorship and technology developed by the employee that relate to the company's business.

An issue that tends to arise relates to invalidity of the agreements for lack of consideration. In general, employee agreements are valid if signed prior to or contemporaneously with initial employment. Some states, however, have held the agreements to be invalid in the absence of some additional consideration to the employee, if entered into after the commencement of employment. This problem is avoided by conditioning a raise or benefit to the employee upon their entering into the agreement.

Non-Competition Agreements

Where particularly critical confidential information is involved, or the employee is in a crucial position, non-competition provisions may be appropriately included. Various states impose restrictions upon the scope of such employee agreements. Non-competition provisions tend to be very strictly construed, and are typically unenforceable if not reasonable in scope as to geography, time, and precluded employment.

Agreements Regarding Third Party Business Relationships

Agreements creating or relating to business relationships with third parties beyond the marketing of products often include provisions that can affect rights in intellectual property or create potential liabilities.

Confidentiality Agreements

A confidentiality agreement is a general term used to describe an agreement drafted solely to impose an obligation of confidentiality on a party with access to confidential information (*e.g.*, proprietary know-how).

If the agreement is well written, it will preclude disclosure of the information and will *also* limit the use of the information by the recipient to a specific purpose, *i.e.*, in connection with the business relationship between the parties. Such an agreement should be in place any time a third party is given access to proprietary know-how, outside of the context of a broader agreement including provisions to impose such a confidentiality obligation.

Consulting and Development Agreements

A consulting agreement may be broadly defined as an agreement under which a third party (individual or business entity) having a particular expertise is engaged to apply that expertise on behalf of the hiring company. The consulting agreement may relate to a particular project of the hiring company or may be more open ended, with the consultant available for any issue involving the consultant's area of expertise.

A development agreement is sometimes considered a specie of consulting agreement where it is specifically contemplated that the consultant (developer) will generate technology. In many cases, the developer is not intimately involved with the operation of the hiring company, and may work on a largely independent basis. There are a number of different approaches to defining the subject matter and administration of development agreements. If a company has sufficient in-house expertise respecting the subject matter of the development, it may itself generate a detailed specification for the item to be developed. Alternatively, a consultant (other than the entity ultimately engaged to do the development work) may be engaged to develop or assist in developing a detailed specification. Alternatively, a detailed specification can be developed by the developer, as an initial phase of the development agreement. Another approach is to issue a more general request for proposals, eliciting proposed specifications from prospective developers. Each of these approaches present different issues with respect to confidentiality and ownership of rights in technology resulting from the work. Compliance issues also often arise with respect to the developer meeting specified milestones, provision of data, documentation and reports called for under the contract, and testing and acceptance of items delivered under the contract.

If well written, the consulting or development agreement will include provisions, which, as pertaining to intellectual property:

> Impose confidentiality (non-disclosure, non-use) obligations;

> Clearly define the scope of the engagement, and all tangible items and documentation to be delivered;

> Define the respective rights of the parties as to ownership of any technology that might be developed during the course of the relationship and rights to preexisting technology incorporated into the developed product; and

> Allocate the risk of infringement of third party intellectual property rights.

In the absence of a written agreement to the contrary, the copyright to any writings or software authored by the consultant or developer will belong to the developer. Likewise, the rights to any inventions made during the course of the engagement will likely belong to the developer, unless the agreement specifies otherwise.

Depending upon the nature and subject matter of the engagement, the agreement may also include provisions precluding the consultant from providing similar services to competitors during the term of the engagement, and for a reasonable period after the termination of the agreement.

Maintenance and Support Agreements

Maintenance and support agreements cover a wide variety of circumstances, but are most commonly encountered in connection with software products. The agreements often involve the provision of updates and error correction of licensed software.

Intellectual property issues tend to arise with respect to ownership and the rights of the licensee to new developments. Issues also tend to arise with respect to representations by the service persons pertaining to the software and availability of updates or error corrections.

Manufacturing Agreements

A manufacturing agreement is a general term used to describe an agreement under which a company hires a third party (vendor, supplier) to manufacture goods (typically a part or component to be used in a company's product) according to specifications provided by the company. The arrangement very often involves communication of confidential information (*e.g.*, the specification). Appropriate confidentiality provisions, and, in some cases, restricted licenses under other types of intellectual property (*e.g.*, patents), should be included in the agreement.

Joint Ventures

A joint venture is a form of alliance of two separate companies; the companies agree to act together, typically forming a separate legal entity, for a particular purpose. In the context of technology transfer, a joint venture can be distinguished from a license in that the owner of the intellectual property actively participates in the enterprise licensed to use the technology. The formation of a joint venture can sometimes provide security to the licensor of intellectual property. Since the licensor is involved in the management of the licensee, the use of the licensed intellectual property can be controlled. This is particularly important in countries which do not have strong intellectual property laws.

Agreements Regarding Sales and Market Relationships

Agreements relating to transactions in the marketplace or creating marketing relationships often include provisions that can affect rights in intellectual property or create potential liabilities.

Purchase Agreements

In general, a purchase agreement is an agreement under which a vendor (supplier) transfers the title to a product to a purchaser (customer). The terms of the purchase agreement are often established by preprinted forms: purchase order, and order acknowledgement or confirmation forms. Issues tend to arise as to the precise terms of the agreement when the terms in the purchase order conflict with those of the confirmation or acknowledgement form. Generally, the contract will be based upon the terms of the order acknowledgement/confirmation form unless the new terms materially alter the crucial terms of the agreement, the terms of the purchase order form expressly preclude formation of a contract under the current terms, or the vendor makes a timely written objection.

In many instances, however, a purchase order will expressly preclude changes in terms, while the responsive order acknowledgement/confirmation form provides for differing terms, and states that a contract would be formed only upon acceptance of the new terms. Often, the individual employees of the parties overlook or ignore the inconsistent positions and proceed in any event with the delivery and acceptance of the goods. Under the Uniform Commercial Code (UCC), that course of dealing does create a contract, based upon the terms that are common to the respective forms, and various other terms supplied by the UCC. Very often, the variant terms relate to warranties (and disclaimer of warranties) and assignment of risks with respect to, among other things, intellectual property right infringement. When this is the case, the UCC implied warranties of non-infringement, merchantability, and fitness for a particular purpose may be deemed applicable.

Distribution Agreements

A distribution agreement can be broadly defined as an agreement under which the owner of a product (manufacturer, developer) engages a distributor to market a product in substantially unmodified form. In some instances, the distributor may install, service, or customize the product for an end user.

Intellectual property issues typically arise with respect to the extent to which, if at all, the distributor is licensed to use the intellectual property of the manufacturing/developing company. This will be specified with particularity in the agreement, if it is well drafted. Where the agreement calls for the distributor to sell the product alone and in unmodified form, intellectual property issues tend to relate to the extent to which, if at all, the distributor is permitted to use the manufacturer/developer's trademarks, and the allocation of risk of liability for infringement of third party intellectual property rights.

Other intellectual property issues tend to arise with respect to distribution agreements involving products which include a software component. For example, where the product is predominantly software, the distributor agreement typically specifies the manner in which the software is to be marketed by the distributor to the end user. Alternative manners of marketing include selling a copy of the software to the end user, acting as an agent for the developer company, acting as a broker for an end user license agreement between the developer company and the end user, or entering into a sublicense agreement with the end user. The substance of a sublicense is typically specified to ensure that the developer company's rights are adequately protected.

Software distribution agreements also tend to present different types of administration/compliance issues. The agreement typically specifies how to generate copies of software that will be delivered to the end user. The copies may be provided by the developer company on an as ordered basis, provided from an inventory maintained by the distributor, or made by the distributor on an as needed basis from a "master copy" provided by the developer company. There are also a number of alternative approaches to providing remuneration to the developer company: a distributor may pay the developer company a preset discounted fee (keeping the difference from fees obtained from the end user) for each copy of the software; the developer company may receive a specified percentage of fees received by the distributor; or the distributor can receive a commission on each transaction, with the fees from the end user going directly to the developer company.

VAR and OEM Agreements

Value Added Remarketer (VAR) and Original Equipment Manufacturer (OEM) agreements are agreements wherein the owner of technology or a product licenses the VAR or OEM to market the technology/product as part of an overall system or product. While there is no standard definition for OEM and VAR agreements, the distinction between the two is often drawn based upon the extent to which the supplied technology/product retains its separate identity. Where the supplied product is a separate module identified to, or identifiable by, the end user, the agreement is typically characterized as a VAR agreement. Conversely, under an OEM agreement, the supplied technology/product tends to lose its separate identity, and becomes an integral part of a product marketed under the OEM's name.

Many of the same intellectual property and compliance issues arise with OEM and VAR agreements as with respect to distribution agreements. However, significant intellectual property issues relating to technology tend to arise more often with respect to the OEM and VAR agreements; compared to a distributor, the OEM or VAR typically has greater access to, and more latitude with respect to the use of, the proprietor company's technology.

The agreement, if competently drafted, also will include provisions allocating risks of liability with respect to defects in the products, and provisions relating to the infringement of third party intellectual property rights. Provisions relating to assignment of risk and cross indemnities are particularly significant in VAR and OEM agreements, and even more so where the VAR or OEM is permitted to modify the supplied product. Indemnity provisions in the agreement often create potential liability on the part of the manufacturer/developer with respect to infringement claims as to unmodified product, and run to the benefit of the manufacturer/developer to the extent that infringement claims relate to modifications of the product by the VAR or OEM.

Compliance issues can be substantial, and tend to arise not only with respect to payment of fees, administration of orders, and deliveries under the agreement, but also with respect to various intellectual property related provisions, such as the use of trademarks, and the extent to which technology is used or modified. Where the product includes a significant software component, the mechanism by which the products are marketed (*i.e.*, sale of copies, brokering licenses directly between the proprietor company and end user, or sublicenses between the VAR/OEM and end user) is also an important aspect of the agreement which often gives rise to compliance issues.

Some Basic Considerations in Negotiating Agreements

Certain basic principles or philosophies are common to the success of any type of agreement.

The Principle of Reasonableness

To be successful, a long term agreement must be fair to both parties. Both parties must benefit from the agreement. If the agreement is unfair to one of the parties, that party will tend to spend all of its energy in looking for some way to escape the agreement, rather than in performance. Never negotiate a license with the idea of "pulling the wool over the other party's eyes." One partner's unhappiness in a marriage leads to the unhappiness of both.

The Principle of Definiteness

To ensure that there is no possible misunderstanding between the parties as to their respective expectations from the agreement, it is imperative that care be taken to carefully and precisely define all terms. This is particularly true where there are cultural or language differences between the parties. Very often a word that is commonplace to one party, which that party thinks is clear and concise, will not have a precise and definite meaning to the other party. Take, for example, the term "exclusive." To a licensor from the United States, an "exclusive" license has a particular meaning. This may not be the case elsewhere in the world. Rather than chance any misconception, it is better to explicitly define all critical terms in the agreement.

The Principle of Completeness

The agreement should attempt to contemplate all contingencies and circumstances and clearly set forth the rights and obligations of the parties in the event that those circumstances arise. Specifically dealing with potential problems that may arise in the future does not imply any particular expectation that those problems will in fact arise, or any lack of trust or unwillingness to cooperate between the parties. It merely assures that the parties have a complete understanding of each other's expectations, and the manner in which foreseeable issues will be dealt with if they occur. This is particularly important where the parties come from different cultures, and may have very different expectations and approaches to dealing with problems.

> Dealing with all potential issues in the agreement does not indicate lack of trust – it ensures complete understanding.

Also, particularly with respect to long-term agreements, the individuals negotiating the agreement, or initially performing under the agreement, may not always be available—those individuals may retire, transfer, or otherwise leave the company. The replacements for the original individuals, who were not a party to the negotiations, may not have the same understandings and may come to different conclusions on the terms or administration of the agreement. To provide consistency of interpretation and order, it is particularly important that the written agreement be complete and include all understandings.

The Periodic Intellectual Property Audit

This handbook has attempted to familiarize the reader with various types of intellectual property, common types of agreements concerning or giving rise to intellectual property rights and potential liabilities, and some of the situations where intellectual property issues tend to arise. Various procedures that can be instituted to prevent inadvertent loss of intellectual property rights have also been suggested.

Intellectual property is becoming increasingly important to the typical successful company. Often, a company's intellectual property is very valuable. In fact, intellectual property may be the *most* valuable asset of a company. Yet, while audits of tangible assets and liabilities are common place, focused audits of intellectual property assets and liabilities of a company extending beyond royalty payment compliance are still a relative rarity.

An intellectual property audit involves more than just compiling the inventory of a company's intellectual property assets. It also involves determining potential liabilities that may be incurred from the use of technology and other items that might be the subject of third party intellectual property rights. An audit also must consider the development of systems and procedures for ensuring that the company's intellectual property is appropriately protected, and infringement of third party intellectual property rights is avoided. Unless appropriate procedures are implemented, loss of rights and third party intellectual property claims can adversely affect the company.

A formal intellectual property audit can be an important managerial tool; up-to-date information on the company's intellectual property assets and potential liabilities can be invaluable to the proper management of a company. It can identify potentially licensable intellectual property of which the company was previously unaware, which could have the ultimate result of increasing the company's licensing revenues. It can also identify potential infringement of third party intellectual property right before the company incurs any liability or, if liability cannot be avoided, in time to control or minimize the liability and perhaps avoid costly litigation. Additionally, contractual obligations can be systematically identified to ensure compliance, and potential disputes and liabilities can be minimized. Perhaps most importantly, an intellectual property audit can serve as a vehicle for establishing procedures to ensure that intellectual property assets are protected and exploited to the fullest extent, and to ensure costly intellectual property liabilities and contractual disputes are avoided or minimized. Thus, if properly employed, an intellectual property audit can significantly and positively impact the company balance sheet.

Conclusion

In conclusion, it should again be stressed that this handbook is not intended to be a definitive text on the various mechanisms for protecting intellectual property. Volumes have been written on aspects and concepts of intellectual property law which here have been allotted only a sentence or two. In many cases, concepts are described in the handbook in very simplistic terms, and many of the ramifications and subtleties involved in the issues are left unexplored. Basically, this handbook is no more than an attempt to alert the reader to various problem areas and to provide a basic understanding of the types of protection available and the procedures by which these protections are obtained.

It is important for a business to be sensitive to "intellectual property" issues. A few relatively painless and simple procedures and precautions can make all the difference with respect to protecting the company's investment in R&D, new products, and developing goodwill and reputation.

APPENDIX I

COMPARISON OF U.S. INTELLECTUAL PROPERTY PROTECTION MECHANISMS

Protection Mechanism	Term	Scope of Protection	Compatible Concurrent Forms of Protection
Trade Secret	Potentially infinite	Protects anything that can be kept secret. No protection against independent development	Trademark
Trademark	Potentially infinite	Protects against others trading on TM owner's reputation – against confusion as to origin of products or affiliation	Trade Secret Utility Patent	Design Patent Copyright
Design Patent	14 yrs. from issue date	Protects ornamental features only	Copyright	Utility Patent Trademark
Utility Patent	17 yrs. from issue date	Protects concept of invention as set forth in claims	Copyright Mask Work	Design Patent Trademark
Copyright	Life of last surviving author and 50 yrs. OR Work for hire: shortest of 75 yrs. from publication/100 yrs. from creation	Protects only the form of expression—not substance or content	Trademark Utility Patent	Design Patent
Mask Work	Until end of 10th calendar year after the registration or first commercial exploitation, whichever is first	Protects against use of reproductions of masks in production of competing chips	Trade Secret Trademark	Utility Patent

APPENDIX II

PROCEDURE FOR PROTECTING INTELLECTUAL PROPERTY

[For Multi-National Concern with Parent and Subsidiary Corporations:
I.P. License in Place Between Parent and Subsidiary]

INTRODUCTION

For various reasons, it is desirable that The Company follow procedures specifically designed to protect The Company's intellectual property in the United States.

The patent laws of the United States have several subtle differences from those of other countries. In view of the peculiarities of U.S. law, and the relative size of the U.S. market, it is generally advantageous to follow procedures specifically designed to maximize rights in the United States. This entails establishing certain activities in the United States at an earliest possible date, and filing U.S. patent applications, specifically drafted with U.S. laws in mind, before, or concurrently with, filing in other countries, rather than base U.S. filings on prior filed applications in other countries. The benefit of the U.S. filing date can then be obtained in selected countries other than the United States by filing in those countries within one year from the U.S. filing date. Accordingly, the following procedures are adopted.

PATENT COMMITTEE

A Patent Committee consisting of a designee for each business group and R&D U.S., and outside patent counsel, will meet at least twice annually on a regularly scheduled basis.

DISCLOSURE PROGRAM AND PATENT PREPARATION

1. <u>Business Group Prepares Concept Report.</u> Upon conceiving an idea for a product, or improvement to a product, a Concept Report should be prepared (and provided to R&D U.S.). The Concept Report should provide as much detail as possible with respect to the contemplated product or improvement (invention), and should be signed and dated. A copy of the Concept Report will be placed in a file maintained under the direction of the representative of the Business Group or the Patent Committee.

2. <u>Business Group Files Concept Report With R&D U.S.</u> The Concept Report, signed and dated by the originators, should be sent to R&D U.S. at the earliest possible date. Upon receipt of the Concept Report, R&D will immediately date stamp, and "witness" the Concept Report, and maintain the witnessed copy of the Concept Report in its files. This procedure will establish the earliest possible conception of the invention in the United States for inventions originating outside of the United States. (Under U.S. law, the date of "invention" can be established only through acts taking place in the United States or the filing of an application for which priority is claimed.)

3. <u>R&D Reviews for Related Efforts.</u> R&D U.S. will also review the Concept Report, and advise the originating business group of any parallel or related projects or developments by other business groups. R&D U.S. will coordinate information transfer and development efforts between the respective business groups.

4. <u>Business Group Performs Venture Analysis.</u> A venture analysis on the concept/invention will then be performed by the originating business group.

5. <u>Business Group Prepares Request Search.</u> Assuming that the venture analysis indicates that the concept should be pursued, a search request disclosure form of the type attached as Appendix III should be prepared. The search request includes, among other things, a description of the subject to be searched (if appropriate, and no further details are available, the Concept Report can be included in this regard as an attachment to the disclosure form), and a list of competitors likely to have similar or competing products.

If the concept is in an area of technology in which searches have been recently performed, the search can be foregone.

6. <u>Business Group Sends Search Request to R&D U.S.</u> The search request form should be sent to R&D U.S. Upon receipt, R&D U.S. will immediately sign and date (witness) the search request, assign the disclosure a docket number, and place the witnessed copy in the file. This procedure provides further evidence of conception in the United States.

7. <u>R&D Institutes Search.</u> R&D U.S. will then provide a copy of the search request disclosure form to patent counsel, together with a request to institute collection and assignment searches.

8. Patent Counsel Conducts Search. Patent counsel will then conduct an investigation to collect relevant patents and, if requested, literature. The results of the search will be provided directly to the business group, with a copy of the letter reporting the search results to R&D U.S. for entry in the file. Patent counsel will maintain a parallel file at its offices.

9. Business Group Reviews Search Results, and Discusses with Patent Counsel. The business group will review the results of the search prior to entering the conceptual design phase of the project. The search results should be reviewed :

   (a) for informational purposes—to prevent reinventing the wheel;

   (b) to identify novel aspects of the concept—potential differences from and advantages over the prior art; and

   (c) to identify potential infringement problems.

Any patents likely to present infringement issues are to be brought to the attention of patent counsel, who will provide guidance as to how to avoid such patents, if possible, and/or consult with business group regarding the desirability of obtaining a license. If there are any questions or concerns, the originating business group will contact patent counsel directly. However, copies of all correspondence to and from patent counsel will be sent to R&D U.S. for entry in the file.

10. Business Group Begin Conceptual Design. Assuming no significant infringement concerns are identified as a result of the initial searching, the originating business group will initiate the conceptual design phase.

11. Business Group Submits Patent Disclosure and Recommendation Form to R&D U.S. As soon as practicable after initiation of the conceptual design phase, *i.e.*, as soon as a conceptual design has been established, a patent disclosure and recommendation form, of the type attached as Appendix IV, will be completed by the business group and forwarded to R&D U.S. The patent disclosure form should be prepared and filed with R&D U.S. whether or not the business group deems the invention to be patentable. The patent disclosure form will include the business group's assessment of the differences from the prior art, and advantages provided by the invention, and a recommendation:

   (a) to file for patent protection, and those countries in which the business group believes patent protection should be pursued;

   (b) not to pursue patent protection; or

   (c) request a patentability opinion.

12. <u>R&D Processes the Patent Disclosure Form.</u> Upon receipt, R&D U.S. will review the patent disclosure form, and the business group's recommendation.

   (a) If the business group recommends that a patent not be pursued, and R&D U.S. concurs, the file will be placed in suspension until the next meeting of the Patent Committee. The disclosure will be reviewed at the committee meeting to permit the other business groups the opportunity to provide input. Unless the committee decides otherwise, the file will then be closed and maintained in storage at R&D U.S.

   (b) If the business group recommends that a patentability opinion be obtained, or if R&D U.S. does not concur in the business group's recommendation, R&D U.S. will request patent counsel to provide a patentability opinion, providing a copy of the patent disclosure to patent counsel. Patent counsel will conduct any necessary additional searching, and render the patentability opinion. Copies of the opinion will be provided to the business group and R&D U.S.

   (c) Upon receipt of the patentability opinion, the business group and R&D U.S. will confer, and R&D U.S. will determine how best to proceed. If R&D determines not to pursue patent protection, the disclosure will be addressed at the next successive Patent Committee meeting. Unless the committee decides otherwise, the file will then be closed.

13. <u>Prepare U.S. Patent Application.</u> Upon a determination that a patent application should be filed, R&D U.S. will request that patent counsel begin preparation of the application. If patent counsel has not already been provided a copy of the patent disclosure form, a copy will be provided at that time. Patent counsel will work directly with the business group in preparing the application. This involves preparing:

   (a) a patent specification which includes (i) sufficient detail to permit the typical person practicing in the area of technology of the invention to actually make and use the invention, and (ii) a description of the "best mode" of the invention contemplated by the inventor at the time of the application, *i.e.*, the most current or preferred version of the invention; and

   (b) one or more claims, defining the scope of the patent.

R&D U.S. will be copied on all correspondence between the business group and patent counsel.

In accordance with the agreement between Parent and Subsidiary, the patent application shall be assigned to the Parent Corporation. The original assignment will be maintained in the R&D U.S. files. Parent Corporation will bear the expense of preparing, filing and maintaining the patents. A ___% royalty will be paid by Subsidiary to Parent on products sold.

14. <u>Patent Counsel Files U.S. Application.</u> After the application is completed, patent counsel will file the application with the U.S. Patent and Trademark Office. Patent counsel will provide copies of all documents filed with the Patent and Trademark Office to the business group and to R&D U.S.

PROSECUTION OF THE PATENT APPLICATION

1. <u>Receive Office Action.</u> After the patent application is filed, the U.S. Patent Office, in due course, takes up the application for examination, and promulgates an Office Action, which either allows, objects to, or rejects the various claims made in the application. The Office Action, in effect, initiates negotiation with the Patent Office as to the scope of the claims. Upon receipt of an Office Action, patent counsel will immediately provide copies to the business group and to R&D U.S.

2. <u>Business Group Reviews Office Action and Provides Comments.</u> The business group will review the Office Action and references cited, and provide patent counsel with its comments.

3. <u>Prepare Response.</u> Patent counsel will then prepare a response, with additional consultation with the business group as necessary. Patent counsel will provide copies of all documents filed to both R&D U.S. and the business group.

4. <u>Further Actions.</u> The foregoing procedure will be followed with respect to any further Office Actions.

5. <u>Protracted Prosecution.</u> In the event that difficulties are encountered in the prosecution of the application, and it appears that a continuing application should be filed, patent counsel will confer with R&D U.S. and provide his recommendations.

PATENT GRANT

1. Assuming the prosecution is successful, a U.S. patent grant will ultimately be issued. Upon receiving the grant, patent counsel will forward the original to R&D U.S., and copies to the business group. R&D U.S. will maintain the original grant in the file.

WORLDWIDE PATENT FILING

1. Within one (1) month of the filing of a U.S. application, R&D U.S. will provide a copy of each application to be considered to each member of the Committee, identifying the originating business group and listing the countries in which the originating business group recommended patent protection be sought.

2. The application will be reviewed at the next successive Patent Committee meeting. In this regard:

> (a) R&D U.S. and patent counsel will present a proposal as to worldwide patent filing for each of the applications. Patent counsel will advise the Committee regarding the likely scope and extent of patent protection that can be obtained. The representatives from the various business groups, and R&D, will provide information to the Committee relating to marketing considerations.
>
> (b) The Committee will then make a decision regarding the countries in which applications are to be filed.

3. Patent counsel will then effect patent filings, if any, in accordance with the Committee directive.

4. Patent counsel will provide copies of all documents filed, and all correspondence pertaining to the prosecution of the applications, to R&D U.S. and the originating business group. Upon grant of a patent, patent counsel will provide the original to R&D U.S. for the central file, and a copy to the operating business group.

Response to Office Actions.

1. The procedure for handling Office Actions in the various applications will be the same as that for U.S. applications.

Maintenance Fees.

1. Patent counsel will maintain an ongoing record of maintenance fees on patents (or subscribe to a commercial service).

2. At the beginning of each calendar year, patent counsel will provide a listing of all maintenance fees coming due during the year to R&D U.S.

3. R&D U.S., after consultation with the originating business group, will instruct patent counsel whether or not to pay the maintenance fee.

4. When a decision is made not to pay a maintenance fee, the issue will be addressed at the next successive Patent Committee meeting (dates permitting) unless the Patent Committee decides to the contrary, the patent will be permitted to lapse.

TRADEMARK DEVELOPMENT PROCEDURES

1. <u>Business Group Reviews Existing Company Marks, Consulting with Corporate Legal and Intellectual Property (IP) Counsel as Appropriate.</u> When considering marks for a new product, an initial review should be undertaken of existing Company marks. The Company has a heritage of trademarks that may be useful for new products. Use of an existing mark with a new product can sometimes save the time, effort, and expense necessary to develop a new mark, and may, in fact, increase the value or strengthen the existing Company mark. (However, where the new product is sufficiently different from those products with which the mark has been used in the past, the mark should be treated as a new mark for purposes of infringement clearance procedures.)

Upon request of the Business Group or Corporate Legal, IP counsel will supply the Business Group with a list of marks used by the Company and the goods with which they are used.

2. <u>Business Group Will Select Proposed Mark(s).</u> After reviewing the existing marks, Business Group will develop a proposed list of marks (existing marks and/or new marks) contemplated to be used with the new product.

When selecting a mark, it is important that the mark be capable of identifying and distinguishing Company products in the marketplace; a trademark must serve the function of identifying the source or origin of the product, rather than identifying or describing the nature of the product. The strength and breadth of exclusive rights in a trademark is a direct function of the distinctiveness of the mark; that is, how closely the mark is associated with the source of the product, as opposed to the nature of the product itself. To this end, coined words with no meaning, or arbitrary words with dictionary meanings that are unrelated to the product, are the strongest trademarks. Since the mark is unrelated to and thus cannot describe any aspect of the product, it can only serve as an identification of source — as a trademark.

There is a tendency, however, to select trademarks that describe the product, its quality, or its function, to convey to the consumer information about the attributes of the product. However, the more descriptive a mark, the less protectable the mark. The marketplace is likely to be cluttered with closely similar marks which dilute the recognition value of the mark, and it is extremely difficult to prevent subsequent unauthorized use of similar marks. The best practice is to choose an arbitrary or fanciful mark to serve solely as a trademark, and provide generic terms on the packaging to provide the necessary information to the consumers.

After the Business Group settles upon a preferred mark or marks, and preferably a number of alternative marks, the Business Group will so advise Corporate Legal, preferably in writing, specifying the marks in order of preference, and identifying with particularity the nature of the product with which the mark is contemplated to be used. Corporate Legal will review the marks suggested by the Business Group for use in connection with the product against existing Company trademarks, and will consult with the Business Group if there are any questions as to the propriety or desirability of using, or not using, existing Company trademarks with the products. If a dispute arises in this regard, Corporate Legal will raise the issue at the next meeting of the intellectual property committee.

3. **Intellectual Property Counsel Will Initiate Preliminary Search.** Once a mark is under serious consideration for use in connection with a product, it is critical that an investigation be undertaken to ensure that no other entities have registered, have applied to register, or are using the mark or a similar mark. Where a number of marks are under consideration, a preliminary search can be performed by IP counsel using commercially available computer databases, to ascertain if other parties have identical registrations or applications pending in the United States Patent and Trademark Office, or in the various individual states. (If foreign distribution is contemplated, consideration should be given to searching the mark abroad at least in key countries.) The preliminary search is useful to eliminate potential marks on the basis of direct anticipations, but is necessarily incomplete, and should not be relied upon as any manner of clearance with respect to the mark.

4. **Immediately File "Intent to Use" Based Applications for Federal Registration of the Selected Trademark(s).** Rights to a mark can be acquired by filing for (and perfecting) a trademark registration based upon a bona fide "Intent

to Use" (ITU). The ITU application should be filed as soon as practical after an intent is formed to use the mark. The filing date of the application becomes the priority date for determining rights to the mark, retroactive as of the date of the eventual issuance of a registration. It is appropriate to file ITU applications on a small number of alternative marks, if it is not clear which will ultimately be adopted so long as there is a likelihood with respect to each of the marks that it will be one of the marks eventually adopted.

It is important that the intent to use the mark be kept strictly confidential until the ITU application is filed. If a competitor learns of the Company's intent to use the mark and files its own ITU application before the Company does, the competitor can coopt the mark.

A request to file an ITU application should be stated as promptly as possible (via telephone or facsimile) to IP counsel, specifying all goods of possible interest (since goods may be deleted later, but not added) and also the anticipated form of the mark. It would be likely, of course, that the design of the label, including the logo for the mark, will not be completed. Accordingly, the application will in most cases have to present the mark in plain block letters, rather than in a fully developed logo. In those few cases, however, in which a logo has already been developed, a crisp black and white drawing of the logo should be furnished to counsel with the request for the application.

IP counsel may expedite the processing by sending the application, perhaps by fax transmission, directly to the officer who will sign it, in his usual location. ITU applications should be signed immediately and returned via fax to IP counsel, so that they may be filed by Express Mail (under appropriate regulations of the Patent and Trademark Office) promptly.

5. Initiate Comprehensive Clearance Search. IP counsel will commission a comprehensive trademark search to help assess the potential strength of the mark and identify any potential conflicting marks. The results of the search will be provided directly to the Business Group, with a copy of the search to Corporate Legal for entry in the file. A copy of the request will be placed in a file maintained by Corporate Legal. IP counsel will maintain a parallel file at its offices.

6. Review Search Results. IP counsel will consult with Corporate Legal, then with the Business Group General Manager and Chief Financial Officer regarding the desirability of adopting the mark, any reservations with respect to the viability of the mark, and/or any third party trademarks likely to present infringement issues. If there is prior third party use of the mark, IP counsel will consult with Corporate Legal, then with the Business Group General Manager and Chief Financial Officer regarding the desirability and likelihood of acquiring

the mark and provide guidance as to how to avoid conflict, if possible, or obtaining some manner of license to use the mark.

The originating Business Group will communicate directly with IP counsel. However, copies of all correspondence will be provided to Corporate Legal for entry in the file.

7. <u>Business Group Begins Packaging Design.</u> Assuming no significant infringement concerns are identified with respect to use of the mark, or reservations with respect to the strength of the mark, the originating Business Group will initiate packaging design. As soon as practicable, the Business Group will provide Corporate Legal with a rendering of proposed packaging. Corporate Legal will review the packaging, consulting with IP counsel as appropriate.

8. <u>IP Counsel Will Prosecute the Application and Keep Corporate Legal Informed of the Progress of the Application.</u> After an application is filed, a Trademark Examiner in the PTO reviews the application to determine whether the mark is, in fact, registerable, that is, capable of distinguishing the applicant's goods from the goods of others. The Examiner also reviews the trademark registration files maintained at the PTO to determine if the mark is "confusingly similar" to any mark already being used by another. Thus, registering a mark and making it available to the Trademark Examiner tends to prevent registration of confusingly similar marks. The results of this examination are communicated to the IP counsel in an "Office Action." A response must be filed within six months of the Office Action.

If decisions must be made in response to Office Actions, IP counsel will communicate these requirements to Corporate Legal, which will process the requests with the appropriate Business Group and send appropriate responses to IP counsel.

FOREIGN TRADEMARK REGISTRATION

1. <u>Business Group Will Confer with Corporate Legal Regarding Desirability of Foreign Filings.</u> In most foreign countries, rights in a trademark can only be obtained through registration. In those countries, with the exception of truly famous international marks (which are the subject of separate statutes in some countries), prior use of a mark does not confer any rights. If a company introduces its products into the country but does not register its trademarks, it is at risk of being preempted by some third party registering the mark. This is particularly true when a company enters into a distribution or license agreement in the foreign country; the distributor or licensee may well end up with rights to the mark. Accordingly, it is particularly important to identify significant markets, and register all valuable trademarks in those countries. The Business Group should confer

with Corporate Legal to determine which countries represent potential markets that are sufficiently significant to warrant the expense of trademark registration and countries where counterfeit goods are likely to originate for export into other markets.

2. <u>Business Group Will Advise Corporate Legal of Potential Distributorship and/or Licensing Relationships and Use Outside the U.S.</u> As previously noted, in many countries, unless the company registers its trademarks, its distributors or licensees may well acquire the rights to the mark in that country. In addition, any agreement that can be construed as a trademark license must include strict quality control provisions. In many instances, the license, and sometimes distributorship agreements, must also be registered to avoid losing rights to the mark and use in foreign countries. Registrations in many foreign countries can be based upon an earlier filed U.S. trademark application. By treaty with many countries, if the foreign application is filed within six months of the filing of the U.S. application, it is as if the foreign application was filed on the date that the U.S. application was filed.

There is also a requirement in some countries that a trademark owner use the mark in that country to maintain its rights. Non-use for a stated period, often two years, is considered abandonment. Use of the mark by a licensee may or may not be sufficient to maintain rights, depending upon the country. Accordingly, Corporate Legal must be kept informed of all usage of the mark outside of the United States.

APPENDIX III   SEARCH REQUEST DISCLOSURE

Title/subject matter of Invention:

Inventors:

        Name: _____
Post Office Address: _____
      Citizenship: _____ Residence: _____
                                 (if different from P.O. address)

        Name: _____
Post Office Address: _____
      Citizenship: _____ Residence: _____
                                 (if different from P.O. address)

        Name: _____
Post Office Address: _____
      Citizenship: _____ Residence: _____
                                 (if different from P.O. address)

Project/Product to which Invention was connected (if any):

Contracts possibly applicable (if any):

Conception date:

First disclosure to others:

    When: Where: To Whom:

Written descriptions/drawings of Invention (if any):

    When: Where: ❏ Copies attached

Any public disclosure/publication (past or planned):

    When: Where: To Whom:

Any potential offers for sale (include all proposals, bids, etc., past or planned):

    When: Where: ❏ Copies attached

Planned use or testing of Invention:

    When: Where: Persons involved:

Description of Invention to be investigated – concept, purpose:

    ❏ See attached

Potentially relevant publications/patents (if any) (identify):

    ❏ See attached

Earlier models/versions (if any):

Differences from known Prior Art:

    ❏ See attached

SIGNATURES:

Inventor	Witness (may be Notary)	Date
Inventor	Witness (may be Notary)	Date
Inventor	Witness (may be Notary)	Date

STATE OF _____)
) ss.
County of _____)

SUBSCRIBED AND SWORN to before me this _____ day of _____, 19____.

                                                      Notary Public

APPENDIX IV   **INVENTION DISCLOSURE**

File No. _____

Title/subject matter of Invention:

Inventors:

                Name: _____
Post Office Address: _____
          Citizenship: _____ Residence: _____
                                          (if different from P.O. address)

                Name: _____
Post Office Address: _____
          Citizenship: _____ Residence: _____
                                          (if different from P.O. address)

                Name: _____
Post Office Address: _____
          Citizenship: _____ Residence: _____
                                          (if different from P.O. address)

Project to which Invention is connected (if any):

Contracts possibly applicable (if any):

Non-Inventors familiar with work on Invention (others working on project, or on Invention under direction of Inventor):

                Name: _____
             Address: _____

                Name: _____
             Address: _____

Conception date:

First disclosure to others:
　When:　　　　　Where:　　　　　　　To Whom:

Written descriptions/drawings of Invention (if any):
　When:　　　　　Where:　　　　　　　❏ Copies attached

Reduced to practice? (Made and tested—list all persons involved, identify all related documents, such as bill of materials, etc.):
　When:　　　　　Where:　　　　　　　❏ Copies attached

Any public disclosure/publication (past or planned):
　When:　　　　　Where:　　　　　　　To Whom:

Any potential offers for sale (include all proposals, bids, etc., past or planned):
　When:　　　　　Where:　　　　　　　❏ Copies attached

Use or testing of Invention:
　When:　　　　　Where:　　　　　　　Persons involved:

Nature of use or test:
　❏ See attached

Brief description of Invention—concept, purpose:
　❏ See attached

Potentially relevant publications/patents (if any) (identify):
　❏ See attached

Earlier models/versions (if any):

Competing products by others (if any):

Problems solved by Invention/advantage over earlier or competing models, Prior Art:
　❏ See attached

Description of Structure/Composition/Process; steps of Invention:
❏ See attached

Differences from Prior Art:
❏ See attached

How Invention solves problem/provides advantages:
❏ See attached

Practical importance of Invention and probable use:
❏ See attached

SIGNATURES:

Inventor	Witness (may be Notary)	Date
Inventor	Witness (may be Notary)	Date
Inventor	Witness (may be Notary)	Date

STATE OF _____)
) ss.
County of _____)

    SUBSCRIBED AND SWORN to before me this _____ day of _____, 19____.

                                                         Notary Public